Microsoft

POWER POINT 7

FOR WINDOWS 95

Gary B. Shelly
Thomas J. Cashman
Marvin M. Boetcher
Sherry L. Green

boyd & fraser

A DIVISION OF COURSE TECHNOLOGY
ONE MAIN STREET
CAMBRIDGE MA 02142

an International Thomson Publishing company I(T)P

CAMBRIDGE • ALBANY • BONN • CINCINNATI • LONDON • MADRID • MELBOURNE
MEXICO CITY • NEW YORK • PARIS • SAN FRANCISCO • TOKYO • TORONTO • WASHINGTON

SHELLY
CASHMAN
SERIES

© 1996 boyd & fraser publishing company
A Division of Course Technology
One Main Street
Cambridge, Massachusetts 02142

COURSE
TECHNOLOGY

 International Thomson Publishing
boyd & fraser publishing company is an ITP company.
The ITP trademark is used under license.

Printed in the United States of America

For more information, contact boyd & fraser publishing company:

boyd & fraser publishing company
A Division of Course Technology
One Main Street
Cambridge, Massachusetts 02142, USA

International Thomson Editores
Campos Eliseos 385, Piso 7
Colonia Polanco
11560 Mexico D.F. Mexico

International Thomson Publishing Europe
Berkshire House
168-173 High Holborn
London, WC1V 7AA, United Kingdom

International Thomson Publishing GmbH
Konigswinterer Strasse 418
53227 Bonn, Germany

Thomas Nelson Australia
102 Dodds Street
South Melbourne
Victoria 3205 Australia

International Thomson Publishing Asia
Block 211, Henderson Road #08-03
Henderson Industrial Park
Singapore 0315

Nelson Canada
1120 Birchmont Road
Scarborough, Ontario
Canada M1K 5G4

International Thomson Publishing Japan
Hirakawa-cho Kyowa Building, 3F
2-2-1 Hirakawa-cho, Chiyoda-ku
Tokyo 102, Japan

ISBN 0-7895-1158-4

SHELLY CASHMAN SERIES® and **Custom Edition**® are trademarks of International Thomson Publishing, Inc. Names of all other products mentioned herein are used for identification purposes only and may be trademarks and/or registered trademarks of their respective owners. International Thomson Publishing, Inc. and boyd & fraser publishing company disclaim any affiliation, association, or connection with, or sponsorship or endorsement by such owners.

PHOTO CREDITS: SoftKey International Inc.

1 2 3 4 5 6 7 8 9 10   BC   0 9 8 7 6

Microsoft
POWERPOINT 7
FOR WINDOWS 95

C O N T E N T S

Preface

Shelly Cashman Series® Microsoft Windows 95 Books

The Shelly Cashman Series Microsoft Windows 95 books reinforce the fact that you made the right choice when you use a Shelly Cashman Series book. The Shelly Cashman Series Microsoft Windows 3.1 books were used by more schools and more students than any other series in textbook publishing. Yet the Shelly Cashman Series team wanted to produce even better books for Windows 95, so the books were thoroughly redesigned to present material in an even easier to understand format and with more project-ending activities. Features such as Other Ways and More Abouts were added to give in-depth knowledge to the student. The opening of each project provides a fascinating perspective of the subject covered in the project. Completely redesigned student assignments include the unique Cases and Places. This book provides the finest educational experience for a student learning about computer software.

Objectives of This Textbook

Microsoft PowerPoint 7 for Windows 95 Double Diamond Edition is intended for a course that covers a brief introduction to Microsoft PowerPoint 7. No experience with a computer is assumed and no mathematics beyond the high school freshman level is required. The objectives of this book are:

> ◆ **More** *About*
> **Design Templates**
>
> You can build a presentation with the default Design Template and later select a different one. When you change Design Templates, PowerPoint automatically updates color scheme, font attributes, and location of slide objects on every slide in the presentation.

- ▶ To teach the fundamentals of Microsoft PowerPoint 7 for Windows 95

- ▶ To provide a knowledge base of Microsoft PowerPoint 7 on which students can build

- ▶ To expose students to examples of the computer as a useful tool

- ▶ To help students who are working on their own

When students complete the course using this textbook, they will have a basic knowledge and understanding of PowerPoint 7.

The Shelly Cashman Approach

Features of the Shelly Cashman Series Windows 95 books include:

- ▶ Project Orientation: Each project in the book uses the unique Shelly Cashman Series screen-by-screen, step-by-step approach.

- ▶ Screen-by-Screen, Step-by-Step Instructions: Each of the tasks required to complete a project is identified throughout the development of the project and is shown screen by screen, step by step.

- ▶ Multiple Ways to Use the Book: This book can be used in a variety of ways, including: (a) Lecture and textbook approach; (b) Tutorial approach; (c) Many teachers lecture on the material and then require their students to perform each step in the project, reinforcing the material lectured. The students then complete one or more of the In the Lab exercises at the end of the project; and (d) Reference: Each task in a project is clearly identified. Therefore,the material serves as a complete reference.

▶ Other Ways Boxes for Reference: PowerPoint 7 provides a wide variety of ways to carry out a given task. The Other Ways boxes displayed at the end of most of the step-by-step sequences specify the other ways to do the task completed in the steps.

Organization of This Textbook

Microsoft PowerPoint 7 for Windows 95 Double Diamond Edition provides detailed instruction on how to use PowerPoint 7 for Windows 95. The material is divided into two projects and one integration feature as follows:

Project 1 – Using a Design Template and Style Checker to Create a Presentation
In Project 1, students are introduced to PowerPoint terminology, the PowerPoint window, and the basics of creating a multiple-level bulleted list presentation. Topics include starting PowerPoint; establishing the design of the presentation by selecting a Design Template; displaying information on every slide; changing text style; decreasing font size; saving a presentation; displaying slides in an electronic slide show; closing a presentation; opening an existing presentation; checking a presentation for spelling errors; identifying design inconsistencies using Style Checker, editing a presentation to correct errors; adjusting line spacing; displaying and printing a presentation in black and white, and, obtaining online Help.

Project 2 – Using Outline View and Clip Art to Create an Electronic Slide Show
In Project 2, students create a presentation in Outline view and learn how to insert clip art. Topics include creating a slide presentation by promoting and demoting text in Outline view; changing slide layouts; inserting clip art; adding slide transition effects and text build effects; running an animated electronic slide show; printing a presentation outline; printing presentation slides in Outline view; rearranging slide order; copying and pasting slides; and, using the Undo button to reverse the last edit.

Integration Feature – Linking an Excel Chart to a PowerPoint Presentation   In this section, students are introduced to the linking feature of OLE by showing them how to link an Excel pie chart to a PowerPoint slide using the insert object method. Topics include linking a chart object to a slide; scaling a linked object; and saving a linked presentation.

End-of-Project Student Activities

A notable strength of the Shelly Cashman Series Windows 95 books is the extensive student activities at the end of each project. Well-structured student activities can make the difference between students merely participating in a class and students retaining the information they learn. The activities in the Shelly Cashman Series Windows 95 books include:

▶ **What You Should Know**   A listing of the tasks completed within a project together with the pages where the step-by-step, screen-by-screen explanations appear. This section provides a perfect study review for the student.

▶ **Test Your Knowledge**   Four pencil-and-paper activities designed to determine the student's understanding of the material in the project. Included are true/false questions, multiple-choice questions, and two short-answer activities.

▶ **Use Help**   Any user of Windows 95 must know how to use Help. Therefore, this book contains two Help exercises per project. These exercises alone distinguish the Shelly Cashman Series from any other set of Windows 95 instructional materials.

▶ **Apply Your Knowledge**   This exercise requires the student to open and manipulate a file from the Student Floppy Disk that accompanies the book.

▶ **In the Lab**   Three in-depth assignments per project that require the student to apply the knowledge gained in the project to solve problems on a computer.

▶ **Cases and Places**   Seven unique case studies allow students to apply their knowledge to real-world situations.

Instructor's Support Package

A comprehensive Instructor's Support Package accompanies this textbook in the form of an electronic Instructor's Manual and teaching and testing aids on CD-ROM. The Instructor's Manual and most of the aids are also available to registered instructors on the Shelly Cashman Online home page (http://www.bf.com/scseries.html). The CD-ROM (ISBN 0-7895-0716-1) is available through your Course Technology representative or by calling 1-800-648-7450. The contents of the Instructor's Manual and additional support materials on the CD-ROM are listed below.

▶ **Instructor's Manual**   The Instructor's Manual includes the following for each project: project objectives; project overview; detailed lesson plans with page number references; teacher notes and activities; answers to the end-of-project exercises; test bank of 110 questions for every project (50 true/false, 25 multiple-choice, and 35 fill-in-the blanks); and transparency references.

▶ **CD-ROM**   The CD-ROM includes the following:

● **Figures on CD-ROM**   Illustrations for every screen in the textbook are available. Use this ancillary to create a slide show from the illustrations for lecture or to print transparencies for use in lecture with an overhead.

● **ElecMan**   ElecMan stands for *Elec*tronic *Man*ual. ElecMan is a Microsoft Word version of the Instructor's Manual, including all lecture notes and the test bank. The files allow you to modify the lecture notes or generate quizzes and exams from the test bank using your word processor.

● **Course Test Manager**   Designed by Course Technology, this cutting edge Windows-based testing software helps instructors design and administer tests and pre-tests. The full-featured online program permits students to take tests at the computer where their grades are computed immediately following completion of the exam. Automatic statistics collection, student guides customized to the student's performance, and printed tests are only a few of the features.

● **Lecture Success System**   Lecture Success System files are for use with the application software, a personal computer, and projection device to explain and illustrate the step-by-step, screen-by-screen development of a project in the textbook without entering large amounts of data.

● **Lab Tests**   Tests that parallel the In the Lab assignments are supplied for the purpose of testing students in the laboratory on the material covered in the project.

● **Instructor's Lab Solutions**   Solutions and required files for all of the In the Lab assignments at the end of each project are available.

- **Student Files**   All the files that are required by the student to complete the Apply Your Knowledge exercises or advanced projects are included.

Shelly Cashman Online

Shelly Cashman Online is a World Wide Web service available to instructors and students of computer education. Visit Shelly Cashman Online at http://www.bf.com/scseries.html. Shelly Cashman Online is divided into four areas:

- ▶ **Series Information**   Information on the Shelly Cashman Series products.

- ▶ **The Community**   Opportunities to discuss your course and your ideas with instructors in your field and with the Shelly Cashman Series team.

- ▶ **Teaching Resources**   This area includes password-protected data from Instructor's Floppy Disks that can be downloaded, course outlines, teaching tips, and ancillaries such as ElecMan and Lab Tests.

- ▶ **Student Center**   Dedicated to students learning about computers with Shelly Cashman Series textbooks and software. This area includes cool links, data from Student Floppy Disks that can be downloaded, and much more.

Acknowledgments

The Shelly Cashman Series would not be the leading computer education series without the contributions of outstanding publishing professionals. First, and foremost, among them is Becky Herrington, director of production and designer. She is the heart and soul of the Shelly Cashman Series, and it is only through her leadership, dedication, and tireless efforts that superior products are made possible. Becky created and produced the award-winning Windows 95 series of books.

Under Becky's direction, the following individuals made significant contributions to these books: Peter Schiller, production manager; Ginny Harvey, series administrator and manuscript editor; Ken Russo, senior illustrator and cover artist; Mike Bodnar, Stephanie Nance, Greg Herrington, and Dave Bonnewitz, Quark artists and illustrators; Patti Garbarino, editorial assistant; Jeanne Black, Quark expert; Cristina Haley, indexer; Debora Christy, Cherilyn King, Nancy Lamm, Lyn Markowicz, and Marilyn Martin, proofreaders; Nancy Lamm, Susan Sebok, Tim Walker, and Peggy Wyman and Jerry Orton, contributing writers; Sarah Evertson of Image Quest, photo researcher; Henry Blackham, cover photographer; and Kent Lauer, cover glass work. Special mention must go to Suzanne Biron, Becky Herrington, and Michael Gregson for the outstanding book design. Particular thanks to Jim Quasney, series editor, whose talents and energy are unmatched in publishing. Without Jim's efforts and dedication, none of this happens.

Gary B. Shelly
Thomas J. Cashman
Marvin M. Boetcher
Sherry L. Green

Visit Shelly Cashman Online at
http://www.bf.com/scseries.html

Microsoft PowerPoint 7 Windows 95

Project 1

Microsoft PowerPoint 7

Windows 95

Using A Design Template And Style Checker To Create A Presentation

Objectives:

You will have mastered the material in this project when you can:

- ▶ Start a new PowerPoint document
- ▶ Describe the PowerPoint window
- ▶ Select a Design Template
- ▶ Create a title slide
- ▶ Change the font size of selected text
- ▶ Italicize selected text
- ▶ Save a presentation
- ▶ Add a new slide
- ▶ Demote a bulleted paragraph
- ▶ Promote a bulleted paragraph
- ▶ View a presentation in Slide Show view
- ▶ Close PowerPoint
- ▶ Open a presentation
- ▶ Use Style Checker to identify spelling, visual clarity, case, and end punctuation inconsistencies
- ▶ Edit a presentation
- ▶ Change line spacing on the Slide Master
- ▶ Display a presentation in black and white
- ▶ Print a presentation in black and white
- ▶ Use online help

Picture This!

A Story without Words

A modern movie without dialogue? The 1981 movie, *Quest for Fire*, contained no dialogue yet told a clear, compelling story about prehistoric humans who had no language to speak. Since the dawn of mankind, humans have relied on graphic images to communicate, even after the advent of spoken language. In today's global village, images play a vital role in promoting understanding between peoples of different languages.

People have long used pictures, or graphics, as guides for building structures involving complex spatial relationships. Imagine trying to build the Pharaoh's pyramids without a plan drawn out on papyrus or a Boeing 767 without engineering drawings.

Yet, in recent years, graphics have assumed an even greater role in the *art of persuasion*. People

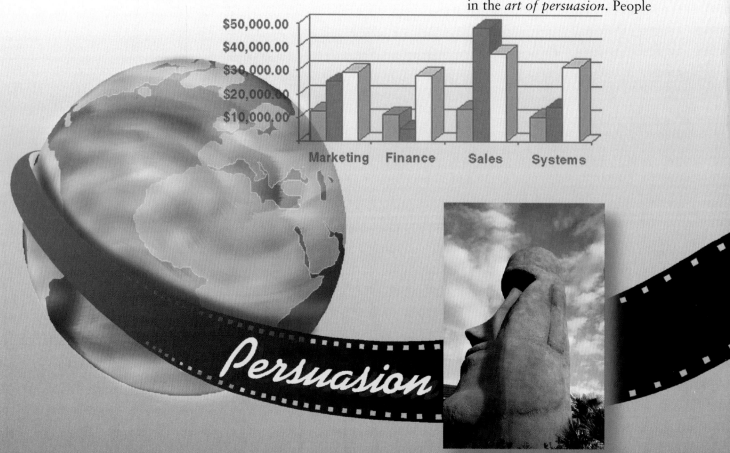

Persuasion

understand arguments far more easily when pictures are used; pictures help establish credibility, which is the first step in persuasion. From sales presentations to the perennial debate over the U.S. federal budget to Presidential addresses, people turn to images to persuade others to adopt their points of view. Human beings grasp information more quickly and remember it longer when images augment words.

It has not always been so easy to create winning graphics. In the past, teams of artists often required days, even weeks, using special equipment many times more expensive than personal computers to lay out slide presentations. Corrections or changes were costly and time-consuming, whereas now, changes can be made inexpensively, in seconds.

Microsoft PowerPoint is an outstanding example of the marriage of pictures and text to help people present persuasive arguments or simply to inform or entertain. Bar graphs, pie charts, scatter diagrams, Gantt charts, and other visuals can be created quickly and easily within PowerPoint or imported from other applications such as Microsoft Excel or Microsoft Works.

For people who need help, Wizards simplify the job of getting started. Wizards provide more than 100 predesigned *looks* and can guide the user through a series of steps to create a unique presentation within one of several popular formats. And it is easy to modify the style, color, and content of all images created with PowerPoint.

PowerPoint can be a boon to students by helping to organize and format papers, prepare overhead slides, and lay out storyboards. Especially where numbers are involved, papers can be enhanced by the inclusion of a graphic from PowerPoint.

In a world increasingly dependent on images as well as language to communicate and persuade, the capability to create those images becomes essential. Who knows what improvements in gradepoint averages may result — with the right graphics presented to the right professor?

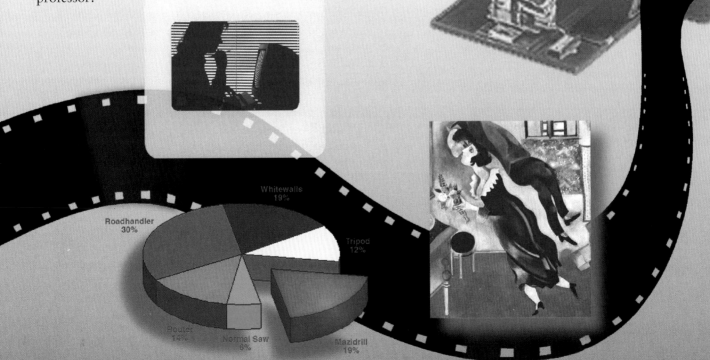

Microsoft
PowerPoint 7

Windows 95

Using a Design Template and Style Checker to Create a Presentation

C*ase* P*erspective*

Each summer, Hammond University conducts an orientation seminar for all students new to the campus. As a new part of the orientation process, the Office of Student Services is conducting a short presentation on how to survive on campus. Ms. Margaret Ray, Director of Student Services, provides you with data and assigns you the task of designing the presentation. Because the location of the orientation session is uncertain, you also must create overhead transparencies.

The data is an accumulation of responses collected each spring from student surveys. The survey focuses on three areas of campus life: dormitory, classroom, and social. Students completing the survey suggest survival tips for each of these three areas. Ms. Ray analyzes the survey responses and identifies the four tips most frequently submitted in each category.

You and Ms. Ray decide the presentation will consist of a title slide and three bulleted list slides.

What is PowerPoint?

Microsoft PowerPoint is a complete presentation graphics program that allows you to produce professional-looking presentations. PowerPoint gives you the flexibility to make informal presentations using overhead transparencies (top of Figure 1-1), make electronic presentations using a projection device attached to a personal computer (middle of Figure 1-1), or make formal presentations using 35mm slides (bottom of Figure 1-1). Additionally, PowerPoint can create paper printouts, outlines, speaker notes and audience handouts.

PowerPoint contains several features to simplify creating a presentation. For example, you can instruct PowerPoint to create a predesigned presentation, and then you can modify the presentation to fulfill your requirements. You quickly can format a presentation using one of the professionally designed presentation Design Templates. To make your presentation more impressive, you can add tables, graphs, pictures, video, and sound; and you can be certain your presentation meets specific design criteria by using Style Checker to locate inconsistencies in spelling, visual clarity, uppercase and lowercase usage, and end punctuation. For example,

FIGURE 1-1

you can instruct PowerPoint to restrict the number of bulleted items on a slide or limit the number of words in each paragraph. Additional PowerPoint features include the following:

▶ **Word Processing** — **Word Processing** allows you to create bulleted lists, combine words and images, find and replace text, and use multiple fonts and type sizes. Using its IntelliSense features, PowerPoint can perform tasks such as checking spelling and formatting text – *all while you are typing.*

▶ **Outlining** — **Outlining** allows you quickly to create your presentation using an outline format. You also can import outlines from Microsoft Word or other word processors.

▶ **Graphing** — **Graphing** allows you to create and insert charts into your presentations. Graph formats include two-dimensional (2D) graphs: area, bar, column, combination, line, pie, xy (scatter); and three-dimensional (3D) graphs: area, bar, column, line, and pie.

More *About* **Overhead Transparencies**

Overhead transparencies are best when you want audience interaction in a lighted room, for groups less than 40 people, or when other equipment is not available.

More *About*
Electronic Presentations

Use an electronic presentation for any size audience. The choice of projection device depends on the number of people in the audience. Be certain you test the system before you deliver the presentation.

More *About*
35mm Slides

35mm slides are best for formal presentations made to any size audience and are highly recommended when audience size exceeds 50 people. 35mm slide presentations are best-suited for a non-interactive presentation because the room is dark.

More *About*
Presentation Graphics

Presentation graphics help people see what they hear. People remember:
10% of what they *read*
20% of what they *hear*
30% of what they *see*
70% of what they *see and hear*

More *About*
Presentation Design

Identify the purpose of the presentation. Is it to sell an idea or product, report results of a study, or educate the audience? Whatever the purpose, your goal is to capture the attention of the audience and to explain the data or concept in a manner that is easy to understand.

- **Drawing** — **Drawing** allows you to create diagrams using shapes such as arcs, arrows, cubes, rectangles, stars, and triangles. Drawing also allows you to modify shapes without redrawing.
- **Clip Art** — **ClipArt** allows you to insert artwork into your presentation without creating it yourself. You can find hundreds of graphic images in the Microsoft ClipArt Gallery, or you can import art from other applications. With the **AutoClipArt feature**, PowerPoint can suggest a clip art image appropriate for your presentation.
- **Multimedia Effects** — To add interest and keep your audience attentive, **multimedia effects**, such as sound and video, can be added to your presentations.
- **Presentation Management** — **Presentation management** allows you to control the design and arrangement of your presentation, as well as add special presentation effects, such as flying bullets.
- **Wizards** — A **wizard** is a tutorial approach for quickly and efficiently creating a presentation. PowerPoint wizards make it easy to create quality presentations by prompting you for specific content criteria. For example, the **AutoContent Wizard** asks you what are you going to talk about and the type of presentation you are going to give, such as recommending a strategy or selling a product. The **Answer Wizard** allows you to ask questions in your own words and then displays step-by-step instructions and visual examples showing how to complete the task. When giving a presentation away from the computer on which you created your presentation, it is important you take all the necessary files. The **Pack And Go Wizard** helps you bundle everything you need, including any objects associated with that presentation.

Project One – College Survival

This book presents a series of projects using PowerPoint to produce slides similar to those you would develop in an academic or business environment. Project 1 uses PowerPoint to create the presentation shown in Figure 1-2. The objective is to produce a presentation, called College Survival, to be presented using an overhead projector. As an introduction to PowerPoint, this project steps you through the most common type of presentation, a bulleted list. A **bulleted list** is a list of paragraphs, each preceded by a bullet. A **bullet** is a symbol (usually a heavy dot (•)) that precedes text when the text warrants special emphasis. The first of the four slides is called the title slide. The **title slide** introduces the presentation to the audience.

Mouse Usage

In this book, the mouse is used as the primary way to communicate with Microsoft PowerPoint. You can perform seven operations with a mouse: point, click, right-click, double-click, triple-click, drag, and right-drag.

Point means you move the mouse across a flat surface until the mouse pointer rests on the item of choice on the screen. As you move the mouse, the mouse pointer moves across the screen in the same direction.

Click means you press and release the left mouse button. The terminology used in this book to direct you to point to a particular item and then click is, Click the particular item. For example, Click the Bold button, means point to the Bold button and then click.

Right-click means you press and release the right mouse button. As with the left mouse button, you normally will point to an item on the screen before right-clicking.

Double-click means you quickly press and release the left mouse button twice without moving the mouse. In most cases, you must point to an item before double-clicking. In this book, **triple-clicking** in a text object selects the entire paragraph.

Drag means you point to an item, hold down the left mouse button, move the item to the desired location on the screen, and then release the left mouse button. **Right-drag** means you point to an item, hold down the right mouse button, move the item to the desired location, and then release the right mouse button.

The use of the mouse is an important skill when working with PowerPoint 7 for Windows 95.

Slide Preparation Steps

The preparation steps summarize how the slide presentation shown in Figure 1-2 will be developed in Project 1. The following tasks will be completed in this project:

1. Start a new Office document.
2. Select a Design Template.
3. Create a title slide.
4. Save the presentation on a floppy disk.
5. Create three multi-level bulleted lists.
6. Save the presentation again.
7. Close PowerPoint.
8. Open the presentation as a Microsoft Office document.
9. Style check the presentation.
10. Edit the presentation.
11. Print the presentation.
12. Close PowerPoint.

The following pages contain a detailed explanation of these tasks.

Starting a Presentation as a New Office Document

A PowerPoint document is called a **presentation**. The quickest way to begin a new presentation is to use the **Start button** on the **taskbar** at the bottom of your screen. When you click the Start button, the **Start menu** displays several commands for simplifying tasks in Windows 95. When Microsoft Office 95 is installed, the Start menu displays two commands: New Office Document and Open Office Document. You use the **New Office Document** command to designate the type of Office document you are creating. Then, you specify the Design Template or wizard on which you wish to base your document. A **Design Template** provides consistency in design and color throughout the entire presentation. The Design Template determines the color scheme, font face and size, and layout of your presentation. Then PowerPoint starts and the specified template or wizard displays. The Open Office Document command is discussed later in this project. Perform the steps on the following pages to start a new presentation, or ask your instructor how to start PowerPoint on your system.

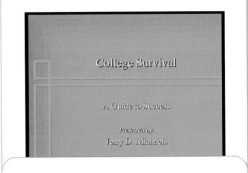
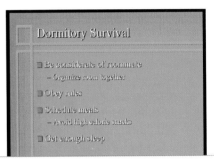
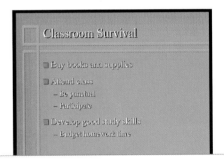
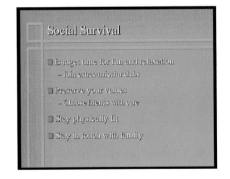

FIGURE 1-2

Steps **To Start a New Presentation**

1 **Point to the Start button on the taskbar at the lower left corner of the desktop.**

When you position the mouse pointer on the Start button, a ToolTip displays, Click here to begin (Figure 1-3). Your computer system displays the time on the clock at the right end of the taskbar.

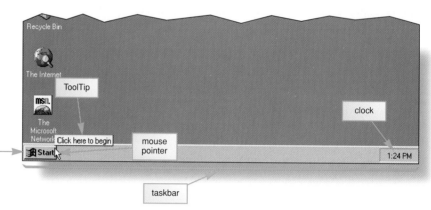

FIGURE 1-3

2 **Click the Start button. When the Windows 95 Start menu displays, point to New Office Document.**

The Windows 95 Start menu displays the names of several programs. The mouse pointer points to New Office Document (Figure 1-4). When the mouse pointer points to a name on the menu, the name is highlighted.

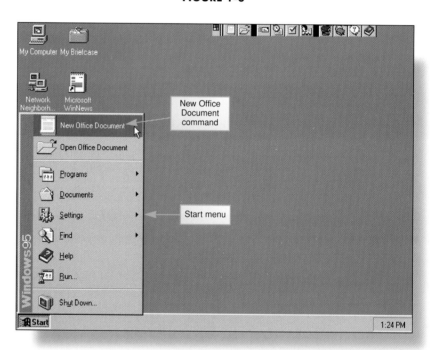

FIGURE 1-4

3 **Click New Office Document. When the New dialog box displays, point to the Presentation Designs tab.**

The New dialog box displays on the desktop and the mouse pointer points to the Presentation Designs tab (Figure 1-5). Depending on your installation, your computer may display a Design tab.

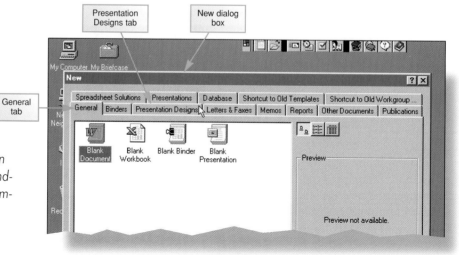

FIGURE 1-5

4 **Click the Presentation Designs tab. When the Presentation Designs sheet displays, point to Embossed.**

The Presentation Designs sheet displays (Figure 1-6). The Presentation Designs sheet displays the names and icons for several Design Templates. The Preview box displays a message about how to see a preview of a presentation Design Template. The OK button currently is dimmed, which means it is not available, because a Design Template icon has not been selected. The Cancel button is available, however, as indicated by the black text on the button. The Cancel button is used to close the New dialog box and return to the desktop or return to the window from which you started.

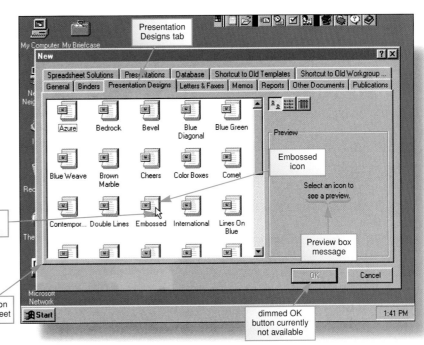

FIGURE 1-6

5 **Click Embossed.**

The Embossed Design Template icon is highlighted and a thumbnail view of the Design Template displays in the Preview box (Figure 1-7). The OK button now is available as indicated by the black text on the button.

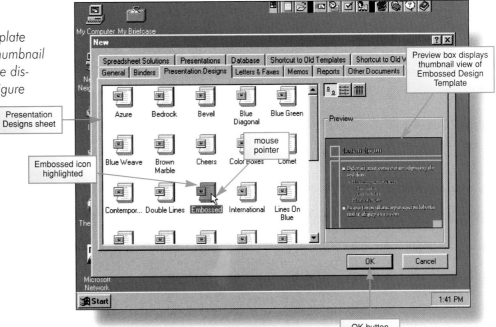

FIGURE 1-7

6 Select the Embossed Design Template by double-clicking Embossed. When the New Slide dialog box displays, point to the OK button.

Double-clicking the Embossed Design Template icon indicates that you are using a PowerPoint template. As a result, PowerPoint starts and the New Slide dialog box displays (Figure 1-8). In the New Slide dialog box, a frame displays around the Title Slide AutoLayout to indicate it is selected. At the bottom of the screen, Microsoft PowerPoint displays as a button on the taskbar.

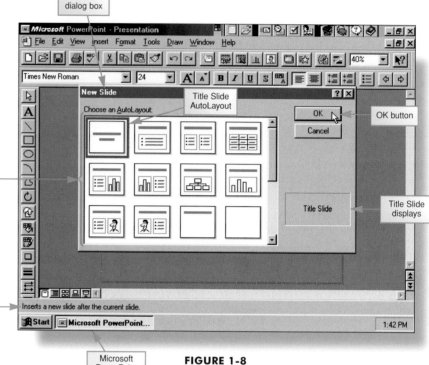

FIGURE 1-8

7 Click the OK button. Maximize the screen if it does not display maximized.

PowerPoint displays the maximized Title Slide AutoLayout and the Embossed Design Template on Slide 1 (Figure 1-9). The title bar identifies this as a Microsoft PowerPoint presentation currently titled Presentation. The status bar displays information about the current slide, such as the slide number and the current Design Template.

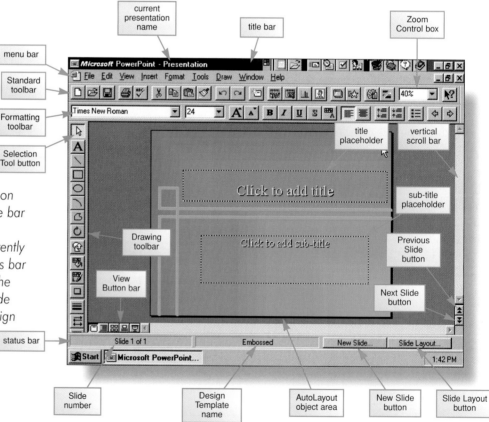

FIGURE 1-9

As an alternative to double-clicking the Embossed Design Template in Step 6, you can click the OK button to apply the selected Design Template.

The PowerPoint Window

The basic unit of a PowerPoint presentation is a **slide. Objects** are the building blocks for a PowerPoint slide. A slide contains one or many objects, such as a title, text, graphics, tables, charts, and drawings. In PowerPoint, you have the option of using the PowerPoint default settings or establishing your own. A **default setting** is a particular value for a variable that is assigned initially by PowerPoint and remains in effect unless canceled or overridden by the user. These settings control the placement of objects, the color scheme, the transition between slides, and other slide attributes. **Attributes** are the properties or characteristics of an object. For example, if you underline the title of a slide, the title is the object and the underline is the attribute. When you start PowerPoint, the default **slide layout** is **landscape orientation**, in which the slide width is greater than its height. In landscape orientation, the slide size is preset to 10 inches wide and 7.5 inches high. The slide layout can be changed to **portrait orientation,** so that the slide height is greater than its width, by clicking Slide Setup on the File menu. In portrait orientation, the slide height is 10 inches and its width is 7.5 inches.

More *About* **Design Templates**

When deciding on a Design Template, choose one designed to display light colored text on a medium to dark background. Light text on a dark background provides a stronger contrast than light text on a light background.

PowerPoint Views

PowerPoint has five views: Slide view, Outline view, Slide Sorter view, Notes Pages view, and Slide Show view. A **view** is the mode in which the presentation displays on the screen. You may use any or all views when creating your presentation, but you can use only one at a time. Change views by clicking one of the view buttons found on the **View Button bar** at the bottom of the PowerPoint screen (see Figure 1-9). The PowerPoint window display is dependent on the view. Some views are graphical while others are textual.

Table 1-1 identifies the view buttons and provides an explanation of each view.

Table 1-1

VIEW BUTTON	VIEW	EXPLANATION
	Slide view	Displays a single slide as it appears in your presentation. Use Slide view to create or edit a presentation. Slide view also is used to incorporate text and graphic objects and to create line-by-line progressive disclosure, called build effects.
	Outline view	Displays a presentation in an outline format showing slide titles and text. It is best used for organizing and developing the content of your presentation.
	Slide Sorter view	Displays miniatures of the slides in your presentation. You can then copy, cut, paste, or otherwise change slide position to modify your presentation. Slide Sorter view also is used to add slide transitions.
	Notes Pages view	Displays the current notes page. Notes Pages view allows you to create speaker's notes to use when you give your presentation. Each notes page corresponds to a slide and includes a reduced slide image.
	Slide Show view	Displays your slides as an electronic presentation on the full screen of your computer's monitor. Looking much like a slide projector display, you can see the effect of transitions, build effects, and slide timings.

PowerPoint Window in Slide View

The PowerPoint window in Slide view contains the title bar; the menu bar; the status bar; the toolbars: Standard, Formatting, and Drawing; the AutoLayout object area; the mouse pointer; the scroll bars; and the view buttons.

More *About*
Presentation Design

The audience determines the level of detail you place on one slide. Before you create your presentation, determine who is likely to attend. Design your presentation around the amount of detail the audience wants to see. Remember, you want to keep their attention, not bore them with details.

TITLE BAR The **title bar** (see Figure 1-9 on page PP 1.12) displays the name of the current PowerPoint document. Until you save your presentation, PowerPoint assigns the default name Presentation.

MENU BAR The **menu bar** (see Figure 1-9) displays the PowerPoint menu names. Each menu name represents a list of commands that allows you to retrieve, store, print, and change objects in your presentation. To display a menu, such as the File menu, click the name File on the menu bar.

STATUS BAR Located at the bottom of the PowerPoint window, the **status bar** consists of a message area, a presentation Design Template identifier, and two buttons: the New Slide button and the Slide Layout button (see Figure 1-9). Most of the time, the current slide number and the total number of slides in the presentation display in the message area. For example, in Figure 1-9, the message area displays Slide 1 of 1. Slide 1 is the current slide, and of 1 indicates there is only one slide in the presentation. When you point to a command or a button, however, the status bar provides a short message about that command or button.

NEW SLIDE BUTTON Clicking the **New Slide button** (see Figure 1-9) inserts a new slide into a presentation after the current slide.

SLIDE LAYOUT BUTTON Clicking the **Slide Layout button** (see Figure 1-9) displays the Slide Layout dialog box. Selecting a slide layout from the options in a dialog box allows you to change the existing layout.

SCROLL BARS The **vertical scroll bar** (see Figure 1-9), located on the right side of the PowerPoint window, allows you to move forward or backward through your presentation. Clicking the **Next Slide button** (see Figure 1-9), located on the vertical scroll bar, advances to the next slide in the presentation. Clicking the **Previous Slide button** (see Figure 1-9), located on the vertical scroll bar, backs up to the slide preceding the current slide.

The **horizontal scroll bar** (see Figure 1-9), located on the bottom of the PowerPoint window, allows you to display a portion of the window when the entire window does not fit on the screen.

It should be noted that in Slide view, both the vertical and horizontal scroll bar actions are dependent upon **Zoom Control**. You control how large or small a document appears on the PowerPoint window with Zoom Control. If you are in Slide view and Zoom Control is set such that the entire slide is not visible in the Slide window, clicking the up arrow on the vertical scroll bar displays the next portion of your slide, not the previous slide. Recall that to go to the previous slide, click the Previous Slide button. To go to the next slide, click the Next Slide button.

AUTOLAYOUT OBJECT AREA The **AutoLayout object area** (see Figure 1-9) is a collection of placeholders for the title, text, clip art, graphs, tables, and media clips (video and sound). These placeholders display when you create a new slide. You can change the AutoLayout any time during the creation of your presentation by clicking the Slide Layout button on the status bar and then selecting a different slide layout.

PLACEHOLDERS Surrounded by a dashed line, **placeholders** are the empty objects on a new slide. Depending on the AutoLayout selected, placeholders will display for the title, text, graphs, tables, organization charts, media clips, and clip art. Once you place contents in a placeholder, the placeholder becomes an object. For example, text typed in a placeholder becomes a text object.

TITLE PLACEHOLDER   Surrounded by a dashed line, the **title placeholder** is the empty title object on a new slide (see Figure 1-9 on page PP 1.12). Text typed in the title placeholder becomes the **title object**.

SUB-TITLE PLACEHOLDER   Surrounded by a dashed line, the **sub-title placeholder** is the empty sub-title object that displays below the title placeholder on a title slide (see Figure 1-9).

MOUSE POINTER   The **mouse pointer** can become one of several different shapes depending on the task you are performing in PowerPoint and the pointer's location on the screen. The different shapes are discussed when they display in subsequent projects. The mouse pointer in Figure 1-9 has the shape of a left-pointing block arrow.

TOOLBARS   PowerPoint **toolbars** consist of buttons that allow you to perform tasks more quickly than when using the menu bar. For example, to save, click the Save button on the Standard toolbar. Each button face has a graphical representation that helps you remember its function. Figure 1-10 below, and Figures 1-11 and 1-12 on the next page illustrate the buttons on each of the three toolbars that display when you start PowerPoint and display a slide in Slide view. They are the Standard toolbar, the Formatting toolbar, and the Drawing toolbar. Each button is explained in detail when it is used.

PowerPoint has several additional toolbars you can display by clicking View on the menu bar. You also can display a toolbar by pointing to a toolbar and right-clicking to display a shortcut menu, which lists the available toolbars. A **shortcut menu** contains a list of commands or items that relate to the item to which you are pointing when you right-click.

PowerPoint allows you to customize all toolbars and to add the toolbar buttons you use most often. In the same manner, you can remove those toolbar buttons you do not use. To customize a toolbar, click Tools on the menu bar, and then click Customize to modify the toolbar to meet your requirements.

STANDARD TOOLBAR   The **Standard toolbar** (Figure 1-10) contains the tools to execute the most common commands found on the menu bar, such as Open, Print, Save, Copy, Cut, Paste, and many more. The Standard toolbar contains a button for setting Zoom Control. Recall that you control how large or small a document appears in the PowerPoint window with Zoom Control.

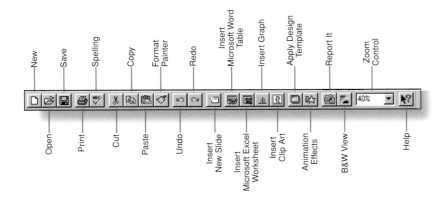

FIGURE 1-10

FORMATTING TOOLBAR The **Formatting toolbar** (Figure 1-11) contains the tools for changing text attributes. The Formatting toolbar allows you to quickly change font, font size, and alignment. It also contains tools to bold, italicize, underline, shadow, color, and bullet text. The five **attribute buttons, Bold, Italic, Underline, Text Shadow,** and **Bullet On/Off,** are on/off switches, or toggles. Click the button once to turn the attribute on; then click it again to turn the attribute off.

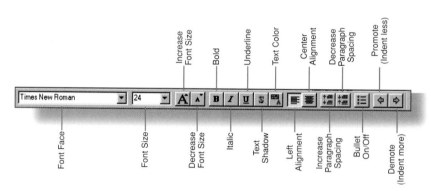

FIGURE 1-11

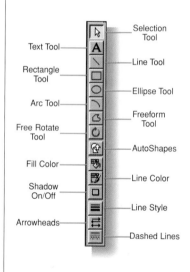

FIGURE 1-12

DRAWING TOOLBAR The **Drawing toolbar** (Figure 1-12) is a collection of tools for drawing objects such as lines, circles, and boxes. The Drawing toolbar also contains tools to edit the objects once you have drawn them. For example, you can add text to an object by clicking the **Text Tool button,** change the color of an object with the **Fill Color button,** or rotate an object by clicking the **Free Rotate Tool** button.

Creating a Title Slide

The purpose of a title slide is to introduce the presentation to the audience. PowerPoint assumes the first slide in a new presentation is the title slide. With the exception of a blank slide, PowerPoint also assumes every new slide has a title. To make creating your presentation easier, any text you type after a new slide displays becomes the title object. In other words, you do not have to first select the title placeholder before typing the title text. The AutoLayout for the title slide has a title placeholder near the middle of the window and a sub-title placeholder directly below the title placeholder (see Figure 1-13).

Entering the Presentation Title

The presentation title for Project 1 is College Survival. Type the presentation title in the title placeholder on the title slide. Perform the following step to create the title slide for this project.

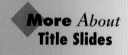

More *About*
Title Slides

To identify a new section in a long presentation, insert a title slide with the name of the new section.

Steps **To Enter the Presentation Title**

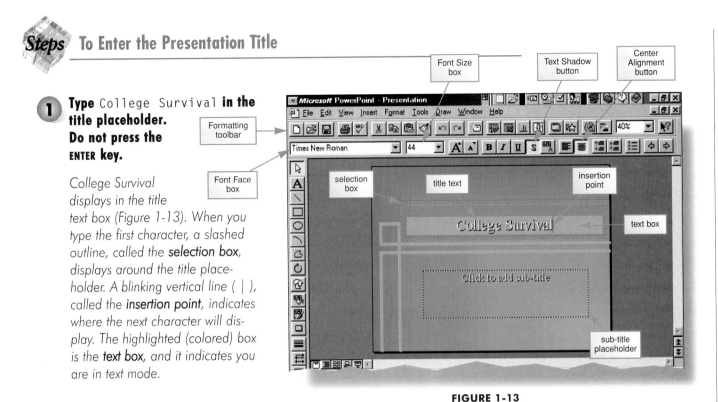

FIGURE 1-13

1 **Type** College Survival **in the title placeholder. Do not press the ENTER key.**

*College Survival displays in the title text box (Figure 1-13). When you type the first character, a slashed outline, called the **selection box**, displays around the title place-holder. A blinking vertical line (|), called the **insertion point**, indicates where the next character will dis-play. The highlighted (colored) box is the **text box**, and it indicates you are in text mode.*

Notice that you do not press the ENTER key after the word Survival. If you press the ENTER key after typing the title, PowerPoint creates a new paragraph. A **paragraph** is a segment of text with the same format that begins when you press the ENTER key and ends when you press the ENTER key again. Pressing the ENTER key creates a new line in a new paragraph. Therefore, do not press the ENTER key unless you want to create a two-paragraph title. Additionally, PowerPoint **line wraps** text that exceeds the width of the placeholder. For example, if the title were College Survival, the Freshman Experience, it would exceed the width of the title placeholder and display on two lines.

The title is centered in the window because the Embossed Design Template alignment attribute is centered. The Center Alignment button is recessed on the Formatting toolbar in Figure 1-13.

Correcting a Mistake When Typing

If you type the wrong letter and notice the error before pressing the ENTER key, press the BACKSPACE key to erase all the characters back to and including the one that is incorrect. If you mistakenly press the ENTER key after entering the title and the cursor is on the new line, simply press the BACKSPACE key to return the insertion point to the right of the letter l in the word Survival.

When you first install PowerPoint, the default setting allows you to reverse up to the last twenty changes by clicking the Undo button on the Standard toolbar, or by clicking the Undo Typing command on the Edit menu. The number of times you can click the Undo button to reverse changes can be modified. To increase or decrease the number of undos, click Tools on the menu bar, click Options, and then click the Advanced tab. Use the up and down arrows in the Maximum Number of Undos box to change the number of undos. The maximum number of undos is 150; the minimum number is 3.

> **More** *About*
> **Presentation Design**
>
> Uppercase letters are less distinct, therefore, more difficult to read than lowercase letters. For emphasis, it is acceptable to use all uppercase letters in short titles. Capitalize only the first letter in all words in long titles, except for short articles, unless the article is the first word in the title.

You can reapply a change that you reversed with the Undo button by clicking the Redo button on the Standard toolbar. Clicking the **Redo button** reverses the last undo action.

Entering the Presentation Subtitle

The next step in creating the title slide is to enter the subtitle text into the sub-title placeholder. Complete the steps below to enter the presentation subtitle.

Steps To Enter the Presentation Subtitle

1 **Click the label, Click to add sub-title, located inside the sub-title placeholder.**

The insertion point is in the sub-title text box (Figure 1-14). The mouse pointer changes to an I-beam. The I-beam mouse pointer indicates the mouse is within a text placeholder. The selection box indicates the sub-title placeholder is selected.

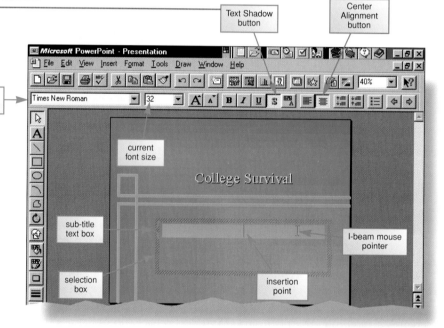

FIGURE 1-14

2 **Type** A Guide to Success **and press the ENTER key two times. Type** Presented by: **and press the ENTER key. Type** J. D. Michaels **but do not press the ENTER key.**

The text displays in the sub-title object as shown in Figure 1-15. The insertion point displays after the letter s in Michaels.

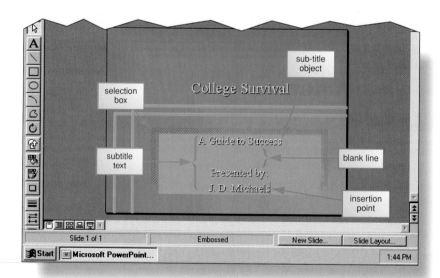

FIGURE 1-15

The previous section created a title slide using an AutoLayout for the title slide. PowerPoint displayed the title slide layout because you created a new presentation. You entered text in the title placeholder without selecting the title placeholder because PowerPoint assumes every slide has a title. You could, however, click the title placeholder to select it and then type your title. In general, to type text in any text placeholder, click the text placeholder and begin typing. You also added a subtitle that identifies the presenter. While this is not required, it is often useful information for the audience.

Text Attributes

This presentation is using the Embossed Design Template that you selected from the Presentation Designs sheet. Each Design Template has its own text attributes. A **text attribute** is a characteristic of the text, such as font face, font size, font style, or text color. You can adjust text attributes any time before, during, or after you type the text. Recall that a Design Template determines the color scheme, font face and size, and layout of your presentation. Most of the time, you use the Design Template's text attributes and color scheme. There are times when you wish to change the way your presentation looks, however, and still keep a particular Design Template. PowerPoint gives you that flexibility. You can use the Design Template you wish and change the text color, text size, text font face, and text style. Table 1-2 explains the different text attributes available in PowerPoint.

More *About*
Text Attributes

Be consistent with color and text attributes. Use bold and italics sparingly for emphasis. Use no more than three type fonts and styles.

Table 1-2	
ATTRIBUTE	**DESCRIPTION**
Font face	Defines the appearance and shape of letters, numbers, and special characters.
Text color	Defines the color of the text. Displaying text in color requires a color monitor. Printing text in color requires a color printer or plotter.
Font size	Specifies the size of the characters on the screen. Character size is gauged by a measurement system called points. A single *point* is about 1/72 of an inch in height. Thus, a character with a point size of eighteen is about 18/72 (or 1/4) of an inch in height.
Text style	Defines text characteristics. Text styles include plain, italic, bold, shadowed, and underlined. Text may have one or more styles at a time.
Subscript	Defines the placement of a character in relationship to another. A subscript character displays or prints slightly below and immediately to one side of another character.
Superscript	Defines the placement of a character in relationship to another. A superscript character displays or prints above and immediately to one side of another character.

The next two sections explain how to change the font size and text style attributes.

Changing the Font Size

The Embossed Design Template default font size is 32 points for body text and 44 points for title text. A point is 1/72 of an inch in height. Thus, a character with a point size of 44 is about 44/72 (or 11/18) of an inch in height. Slide 1 requires you to decrease the font size for the paragraph, Presented by:. Perform the steps on the next pages to change font size.

Steps   To Decrease Font Size

1 **Triple-click the paragraph, Presented by:, in the sub-title object.**

The paragraph, Presented by:, is highlighted (Figure 1-16).

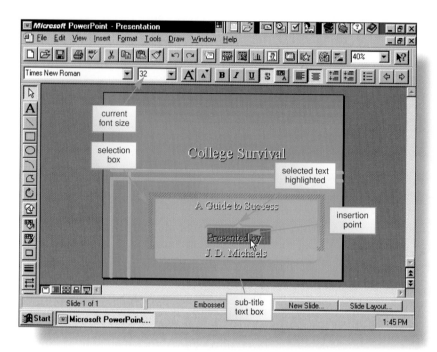

FIGURE 1-16

2 **With Presented by: highlighted, point to the Decrease Font Size button on the Formatting toolbar.**

*When you point to a button on a toolbar, PowerPoint displays a ToolTip. A **ToolTip** contains the name of the tool to which you are pointing. When pointing to the **Decrease Font Size button**, the ToolTip displays the words, Decrease Font Size (Figure 1-17).*

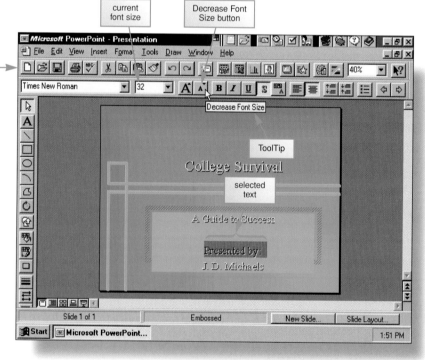

FIGURE 1-17

3 **Click the Decrease Font Size button twice so that 24 displays in the Font Size box on the Formatting toolbar.**

The paragraph, Presented by:, reduces to 24 points (Figure 1-18). The Font Size box displays the new font size as 24.

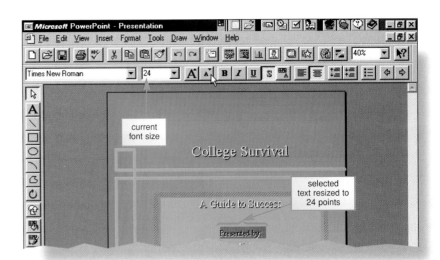

FIGURE 1-18

If you need to increase the font size, click the **Increase Font size button**, located immediately to the left of the Decrease Font Size button on the Formatting toolbar.

Changing the Style of Text to Italic

Text styles include plain, italic, bold, shadowed, and underlined. PowerPoint allows you to use one or more text styles in your presentation. Perform the following steps to add emphasis to the title slide by changing plain text to italic text.

 Steps To Change the Text Style to Italic

1 **With the paragraph, Presented by:, highlighted, click the Italic button on the Formatting toolbar.**

The text is italicized and the Italic button is recessed (Figure 1-19).

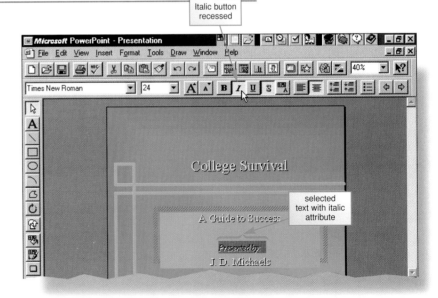

FIGURE 1-19

Other Ways

1. Right-click selected text, click Font on shortcut menu, click new font size in Size list box
2. Click Font Size arrow on Formatting toolbar, click one of listed font sizes, or click Font Size box on Formatting toolbar, type font size between 1 and 4000
3. On Format menu click Font, click new font size in Size list box

Other Ways

1. Right-click selected text, click Font on shortcut menu, click Italic in Font Style list box
2. On Format menu click Font, click Italic in Font Style list box
3. Press CTRL+I

More *About*
Saving

Before you make extreme changes to your presentation, save a copy of it with a different filename using the Save As command on the File menu. This way, if you decide you do not like the new version, you will still have a copy of the original presentation.

To remove italics from text, select the italicized text and then click the Italic button. As a result, the Italic button is not recessed and the text does not have the italic font style.

Saving a Presentation to a Floppy Disk

While you are building your presentation, the computer stores it in main memory. It is important to save your presentation frequently because, if the computer is turned off or you lose electrical power, the presentation is lost. Another reason to save your work is that if you run out of lab time before completing your project, you may finish the project later without having to start over. Therefore, you must save any presentation you will use later. Before you continue with Project 1, save the work completed thus far. Perform the following steps to save a presentation to a floppy disk in drive A using the Save button on the Standard toolbar.

To Save a Presentation to a Floppy Disk

1 **Insert a formatted floppy disk in drive A. Then click the Save button on the Standard toolbar.**

The File Save dialog displays (Figure 1-20). The insertion point displays in the File name drop-down list box. The default folder, My Documents, displays in the Save in drop-down list box. Presentations displays in the Save as type drop-down list box. The Save button is dimmed (not available) because you have not yet entered a name in the File name drop-down list box. The Cancel button is available, as indicated by the black text on the button. Clicking the Cancel button closes the File Save dialog box and returns to the PowerPoint window.

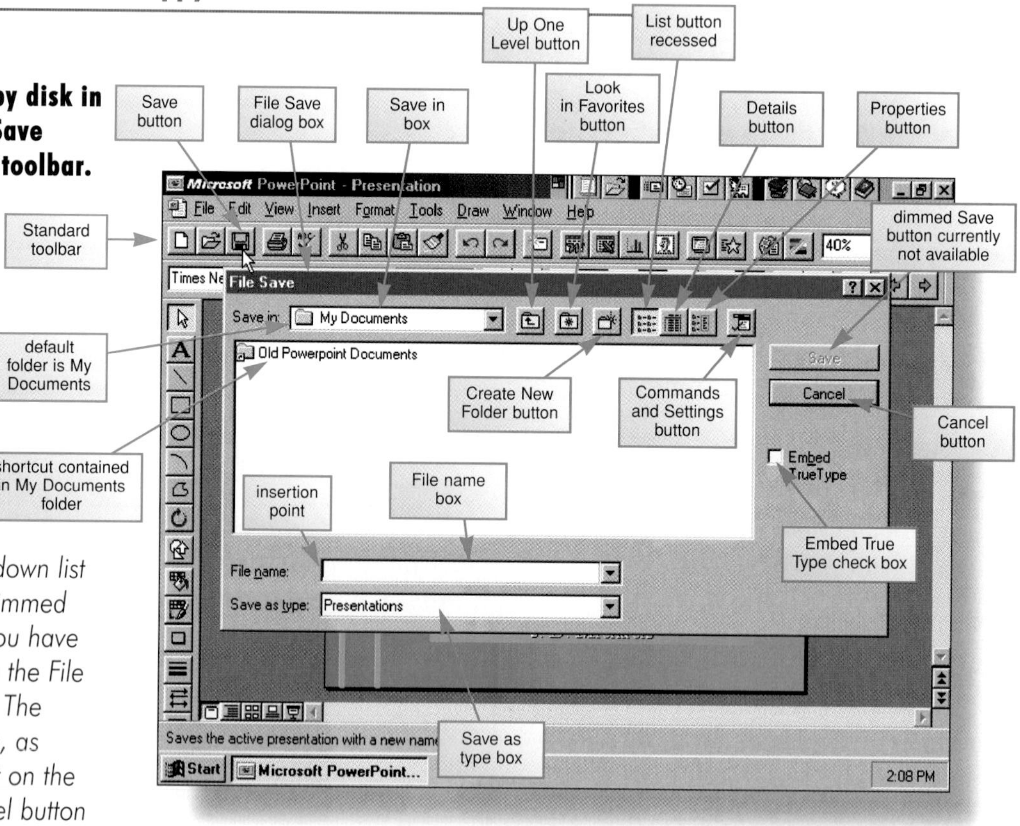

FIGURE 1-20

2 **Type** College Survival **in the File name box. Do not press the ENTER key after typing the filename. Click the Save in box arrow.**

The name, College Survival, displays in the File name drop-down list box. The Save in drop-down list box displays a list of locations to which you can save your presentation (Figure 1-21). Your list may look different depending on the configuration of your system. The black text on the Save button indicates it is available.

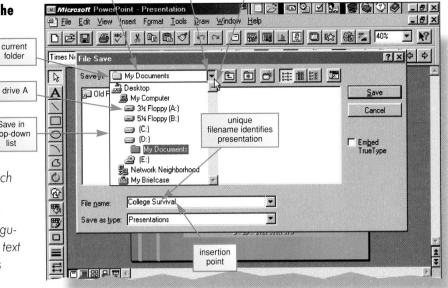

FIGURE 1-21

3 **Point to 3½ Floppy [A:] in the Save in drop-down list.**

3½ Floppy [A:] is highlighted (Figure 1-22).

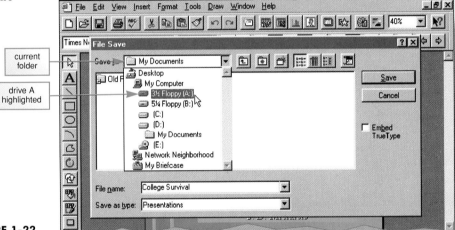

FIGURE 1-22

4 **Click 3½ Floppy [A:]. Then point to the Save button.**

Drive A becomes the current drive (Figure 1-23).

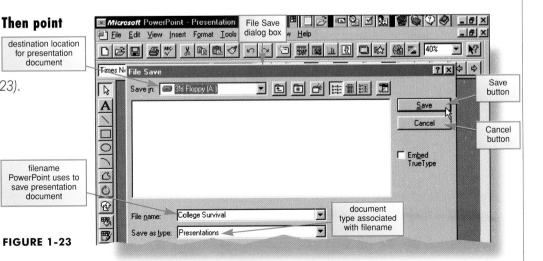

FIGURE 1-23

5 **Click the Save button.**

PowerPoint saves the presentation to your data floppy disk in drive A. Slide 1 displays in Slide view. The title bar displays College Survival, the filename used to save the presentation (Figure 1-24).

filename displays in title bar

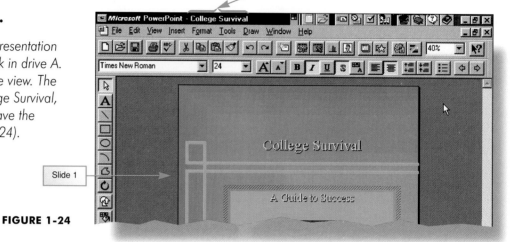

Slide 1

FIGURE 1-24

OtherWays
1. On File menu click Save
2. Press CTRL+S or press SHIFT+F12

PowerPoint automatically appends to the filename, College Survival, the extension **.ppt**, which stands for **P**ower**P**oint. Although the presentation, College Survival, is saved on a floppy disk, it also remains in main memory and displays on the screen.

It is a good practice to save periodically while you are working on a project. By doing so, you protect yourself from losing all the work you have done since the last time you saved.

Adding a New Slide to a Presentation

The title slide for your presentation is created. The next step is to add the first bulleted list slide in Project 1. Clicking the New Slide button on the status bar adds a slide into the presentation immediately after the current slide. Usually when you create your presentation, you are adding slides with text, graphics, or charts. When you add a new slide, PowerPoint displays a dialog box for you to choose one of the AutoLayouts. These AutoLayouts have placeholders for various objects, such as a title, text, graphics, graphs, and charts. Some placeholders provide access to other PowerPoint objects by allowing you to double-click the placeholder. Figure 1-25 displays the twenty-four different AutoLayouts available in PowerPoint. More information about using Auto-Layout placeholders to add graphics follows in subsequent projects. Perform the following steps to add a new slide using the Bulleted List AutoLayout.

Bulleted List AutoLayout

twenty-four different AutoLayouts

Title Slide	Bulleted List	2 Column Text	Table
Text & Graph	Graph & Text	Organization Chart	Graph
Text & Clip Art	Clip Art & Text	Title Only	Blank
Text & Object	Object & Text	Large Object	Object
Text & Media Clip	Media Clip & Text	Object over Text	Text over Object
Text & 2 Objects	2 Objects & Text	2 Objects over Text	4 Objects

FIGURE 1-25

Steps To Add a New Slide Using the Bulleted List AutoLayout

1 Point to the New Slide button on the status bar (Figure 1-26).

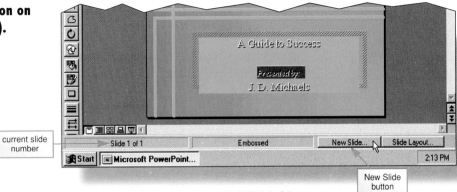

FIGURE 1-26

2 Click the New Slide button. When the New Slide dialog box displays, point to the OK button.

The New Slide dialog box displays (Figure 1-27). The Bulleted List AutoLayout is selected and the AutoLayout title, Bulleted List, displays at the bottom right corner of the New Slide dialog box.

FIGURE 1-27

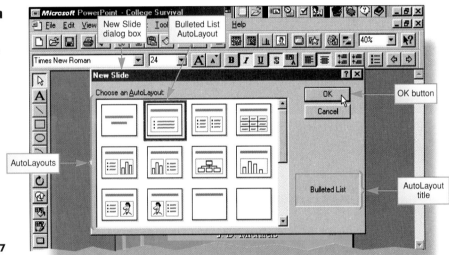

3 Click the OK button.

Slide 2 displays, keeping the attributes of the Embossed Design Template (Figure 1-28). Slide 2 of 2 displays on the status bar.

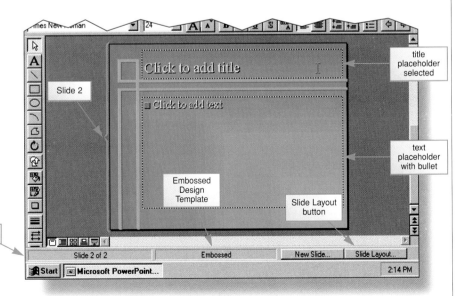

Other Ways

1. Click Insert New Slide button on Standard toolbar

2. On Insert menu click New Slide

3. Press CTRL+ENTER or press CTRL+M

FIGURE 1-28

Because you selected the Bulleted List AutoLayout, PowerPoint displays Slide 2 with a title placeholder and a text placeholder with a bullet. You can change the layout for a slide at any time during the creation of your presentation by clicking the Layout button on the status bar and then double-clicking the AutoLayout of your choice.

Creating a Bulleted List Slide

The bulleted list slides in Figure 1-2 on page PP 1.9, contain more than one level of bulleted text. A slide with more than one level of bulleted text is called a **multi-level bulleted list slide**. A **level** is a position within a structure, such as an outline, that indicates a magnitude of importance. PowerPoint allows for five paragraph levels. Each paragraph level has an associated bullet. The bullet font is dependent on the Design Template. Figure 1-29 identifies the five paragraph levels and the bullet fonts for the Embossed Design Template. Beginning with the Second Level, each paragraph indents .5 inch to the right of the preceding level. For example, the Level Two paragraph indents .5 inch to the right of the Level One paragraph. The Level Three paragraph indents .5 inch to the right of the Level Two paragraph or 1 inch to the right of the Level One paragraph.

An indented paragraph is said to be **demoted**, or pushed down to a lower level. For example, if you demote a First Level paragraph, it becomes a Second Level paragraph. This lower level paragraph is a subset of the higher level paragraph. It usually contains information that supports the topic in the paragraph immediately above it. You demote a paragraph by clicking the **Demote (Indent more) button** on the Formatting toolbar.

When you want to raise a paragraph from a lower level to a higher level, you **promote** the paragraph by clicking the **Promote (Indent less) button** on the Formatting toolbar.

Creating a multi-level bulleted list slide requires several steps. Initially, you enter a slide title. Next, you select a text placeholder. Then you type the text for the multi-level bulleted list, demoting and promoting paragraphs as needed. The next several sections explain how to add a multi-level bulleted list slide.

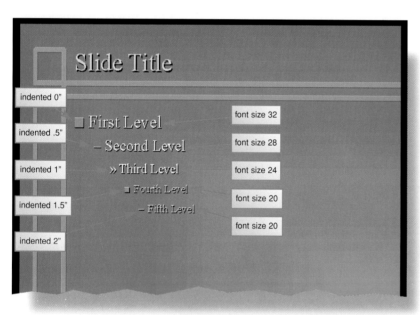

FIGURE 1-29

Entering a Slide Title

PowerPoint assumes every new slide has a title. Therefore, any text you type after a new slide displays becomes the title object. The title for Slide 2 is Dormitory Survival. Perform the following step to enter this title.

 **To Enter a Slide Title**

① **Type** Dormitory Survival **in the title placeholder. Do not press the ENTER key.**

The title, Dormitory Survival, displays in the title object (Figure 1-30). The insertion point displays after the I in Survival.

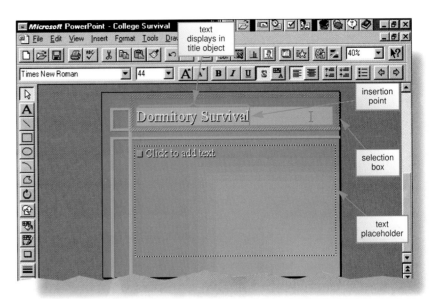

FIGURE 1-30

Selecting a Text Placeholder

Before you can type text into the text placeholder, you must first select it. Perform the following step to select the text placeholder on Slide 2.

 To Select A Text Placeholder

① **Click the bulleted paragraph labeled, Click to add text.**

The insertion point displays immediately after the bullet on Slide 2 (Figure 1-31). The Bullet On/Off button is recessed.

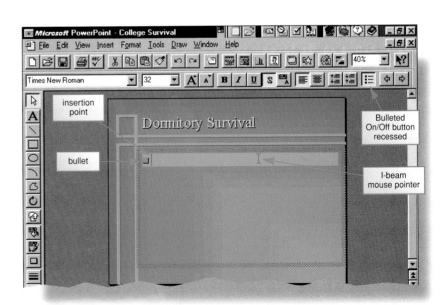

FIGURE 1-31

1. Press CTRL+ENTER

Typing a Multi-level Bulleted List

Recall that a bulleted list is a list of paragraphs, each of which is preceded by a bullet. Also recall that a paragraph is a segment of text ended by pressing the ENTER key. The next step is to type the multi-level bulleted list, which consists of the six entries shown in Figure 1-2 on page PP 1.9. Perform the following steps to type a multi-level bulleted list.

Steps To Type a Multi-level Bulleted List

1 **Type** Be considerate of roommate **and press the ENTER key.**

The paragraph, Be considerate of roommate, displays. The font size is 32. The insertion point displays after the second bullet (Figure 1-32). When you press the ENTER key, the word processing feature of PowerPoint marks the end of one paragraph and begins a new paragraph. Because you are using the Bulleted List AutoLayout, PowerPoint places a bullet in front of the new paragraph.

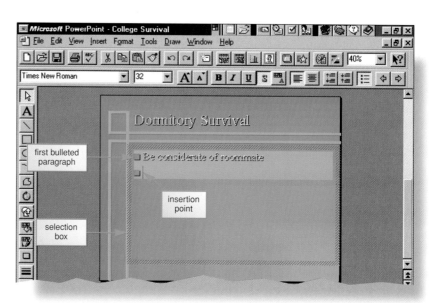

FIGURE 1-32

2 **Point to the Demote (Indent more) button on the Formatting toolbar (Figure 1-33).**

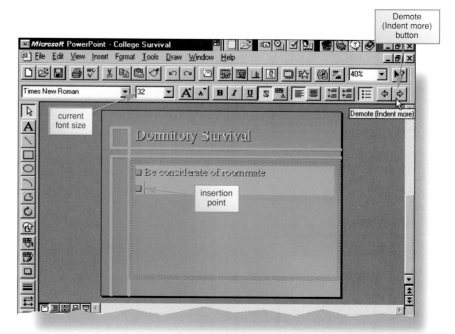

FIGURE 1-33

3 **Click the Demote (Indent more) button.**

The second paragraph indents under the first and becomes a Second Level paragraph (Figure 1-34). Notice the bullet in front of the second paragraph changes from a block to a dash and the font size for the demoted paragraph is now 28. The insertion point displays after the dash.

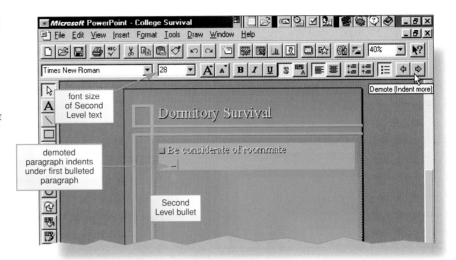

FIGURE 1-34

4 **Type** Organize room together **and press the ENTER key.**

A new Second Level paragraph displays with a dash bullet (Figure 1-35). When you press the ENTER key, PowerPoint adds a new paragraph at the same level as the previous paragraph.

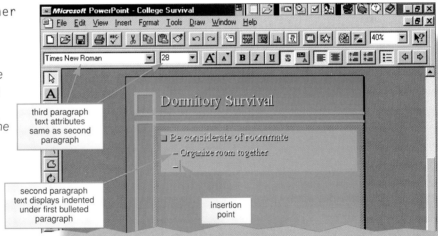

FIGURE 1-35

5 **Point to the Promote (Indent less) button on the Formatting toolbar (Figure 1-36).**

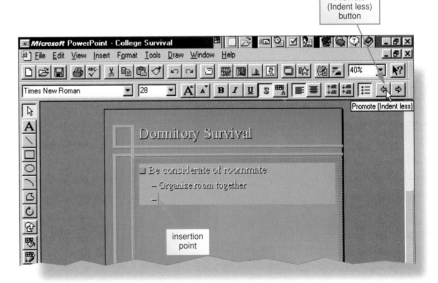

FIGURE 1-36

6 **Click the Promote (Indent less) button.**

The Second Level paragraph becomes a First Level paragraph (Figure 1-37). Notice the bullet in front of the new paragraph changes from a dash to a block and the font size for the promoted paragraph is 32. The insertion point displays after the block bullet.

FIGURE 1-37

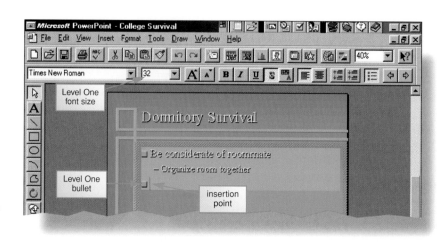

Perform the following steps to complete the text for Slide 2.

TO TYPE THE REMAINING TEXT FOR SLIDE 2

Step 1: Type Obey rules and press the ENTER key.
Step 2: Type Schedule meals and press the ENTER key.
Step 3: Click the Demote (Indent more) button.
Step 4: Type Avoid high calorie snacks and press the ENTER key.
Step 5: Click the Promote (Indent less) button.
Step 6: Type Get enough sleep but do not press the ENTER key.

The insertion point displays after the p in sleep (Figure 1-38).

Notice that you did not press the ENTER key after typing the last paragraph in Step 6. If you press the ENTER key, a new bullet displays after the last entry on this slide. To remove an extra bullet, press the BACKSPACE key.

Adding a New Slide with the Same AutoLayout

When you add a new slide to a presentation and want to keep the same AutoLayout used on the previous slide, PowerPoint gives you a shortcut. Instead of clicking the New Slide button and clicking an AutoLayout in the New Slide dialog box, you can press and hold down the SHIFT key and click the New Slide button. Perform the following step to add a new slide (Slide 3) and keep the Bulleted List AutoLayout used on the previous slide.

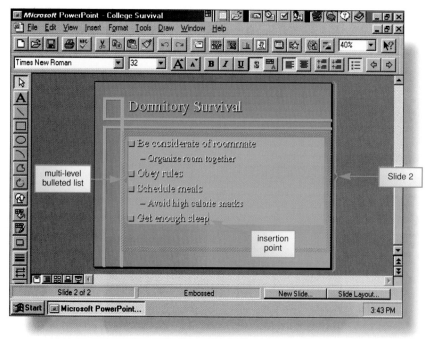

FIGURE 1-38

Steps To Add a New Slide with the Same AutoLayout

1 **Press and hold down the SHIFT key. Click the New Slide button on the status bar. Then release the SHIFT key.**

Slide 3 displays with the Bulleted List AutoLayout (Figure 1-39). Slide 3 of 3 displays on the status bar.

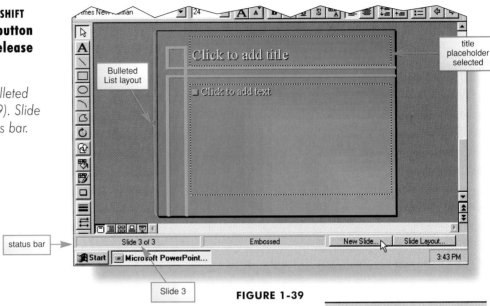

FIGURE 1-39

OtherWays

1. Press SHIFT+CTRL+M

Slide 3 is added to the presentation. Perform the following steps to add text to Slide 3 and create a multi-level bulleted list.

TO CREATE SLIDE 3

Step 1: Type Classroom Survival in the title placeholder.
Step 2: Click the text placeholder.
Step 3: Type Learn your way around campus and press the ENTER key.
Step 4: Type Buy books and supplies and press the ENTER key.
Step 5: Type Attend class and press the ENTER key.
Step 6: Click the Demote (Indent more) button. Then type Be punctual and press the ENTER key.
Step 7: Type Participate and press the ENTER key.
Step 8: Click the Promote (Indent less) button. Then type Develop good study skills and press the ENTER key.
Step 9: Click the Demote (Indent more) button. Then type Budget homework time but do not press the ENTER key.

Slide 3 displays as shown in Figure 1-40.

Slide 4 is the last slide in this presentation. It, too, is a multi-level bulleted list. Perform the steps on the next page to create Slide 4.

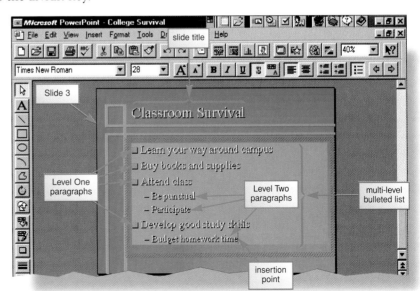

FIGURE 1-40

TO CREATE SLIDE 4

Step 1: Press and hold down the SHIFT key and click the New Slide button on the status bar. Release the SHIFT key.
Step 2: Type Social Survival in the title placeholder.
Step 3: Click the text placeholder.
Step 4: Type Budget time for fun and relaxation and press the ENTER key.
Step 5: Click the Demote (Indent more) button. Then type Join extracurricular clubs and press the ENTER key.
Step 6: Click the Promote (Indent less) button. Then type Preserve your values and press the ENTER key.
Step 7: Click the Demote (Indent more) button. Then type Choose friends with care and press the ENTER key.
Step 8: Click the Promote (Indent less) button. Then type Stay physically fit and press the ENTER key.
Step 9: Type Stay in touch with family but do not press the ENTER key.

The slide title and text object display as shown in Figure 1-41.

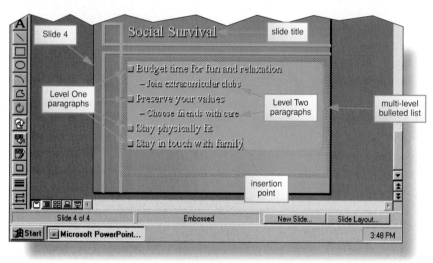

FIGURE 1-41

All slides for the College Survival presentation are created. This presentation consists of a title slide and three multi-level bulleted list slides.

Saving a Presentation with the Same Filename

Saving frequently never can be overemphasized. When you first saved the presentation, you clicked the Save button on the Standard toolbar and the File Save dialog box displayed. When you want to save the changes made to the presentation after your last save, you again click the Save button. This time, however, the File Save dialog box does not display because PowerPoint updates the document called College Survival.ppt on your data floppy disk. Perform the following steps to save the presentation again.

TO SAVE A PRESENTATION WITH THE SAME FILENAME

Step 1: Be sure your data floppy disk is in drive A.
Step 2: Click the Save button on the Standard toolbar.

PowerPoint overwrites the old College Survival.ppt document on the data floppy disk in drive A with the revised presentation document, College Survival.ppt. Slide 4 displays in the PowerPoint window.

Moving to Another Slide in Slide View

When creating or editing a presentation in Slide view, you often want to display a slide other than the current one. Dragging the vertical scroll bar box up or down moves you through your presentation. The box on the vertical scroll bar is called the **elevator** and is shown in Figure 1-42. When you drag the elevator, the **slide indicator** displays the number and the title of the slide you are about to display. Releasing the mouse button displays the slide.

Using the Vertical Scroll Bar to Move to Another Slide

Before continuing with Project 1, you want to display the title slide. Perform the following steps to move from Slide 4 to the Slide 1 using the vertical scroll bar.

Other Ways

1. Click Next Slide button on vertical scroll bar to move forward one slide, or click Previous Slide button on the vertical scroll bar to move back one slide

2. Press PAGE DOWN to move forward one slide, or press PAGE UP to move back one slide

Steps To Use the Vertical Scroll Bar to Move to Another Slide

1 **Position the mouse pointer on the elevator. Press and hold down the left mouse button.**

Slide: 4, Social Survival, displays in the slide indicator (Figure 1-42).

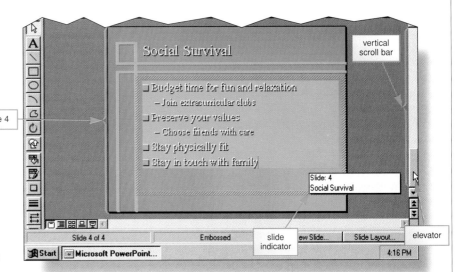

FIGURE 1-42

2 **Drag the elevator up the vertical scroll bar until Slide: 1 College Survival displays in the slide indicator.**

Slide: 1, College Survival, displays in the slide indicator. Slide 4 still displays in the PowerPoint window (Figure 1-43).

3 **Release the left mouse button.**

Slide 1, titled College Survival, displays in the PowerPoint window.

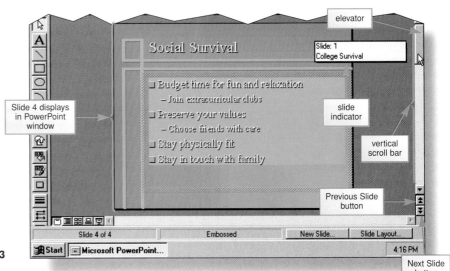

FIGURE 1-43

Viewing the Presentation Using Slide Show

The **Slide Show button**, located at the bottom left of the PowerPoint window, allows you to display your presentation electronically using a computer. The computer acts like a slide projector, displaying each slide on a full screen. The full screen slide hides the toolbars, menus, and other PowerPoint window elements.

Starting Slide Show View

Slide Show view begins when you click the Slide Show button. PowerPoint then displays the current slide on the full screen without any of the PowerPoint window objects, such as the menu bar or toolbars. Perform the following steps to start Slide Show view.

 Steps To Start Slide Show View

1 **Point to the Slide Show button on the View Button bar.**

The Slide View button is recessed because you are still in Slide view (Figure 1-44).

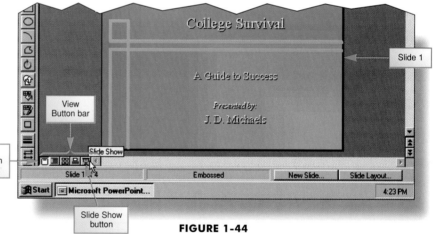

FIGURE 1-44

2 **Click the Slide Show button.**

The title slide fills the screen (Figure 1-45). The PowerPoint window is hidden.

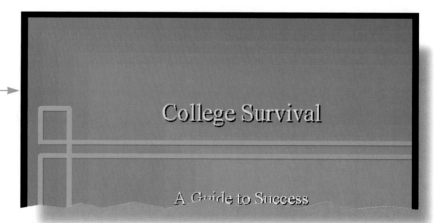

FIGURE 1-45

Other Ways

1. On View menu click Slide Show

Advancing through a Slide Show Manually

After you begin Slide Show view, you can move forward or backward through your slides. PowerPoint allows you to advance through your slides manually or automatically. Automatic advancing is discussed in a later project. Perform the step below to manually move through your slides.

 Steps To Manually Move Through Slides in a Slide Show

Slide 4 in Slide Show view

 1 **Click each slide until the last slide of the presentation, Slide 4, Social Survival, displays.**

Each slide in your presentation displays on the screen, one slide at a time. Each time you click the mouse button, the next slide displays (Figure 1-46).

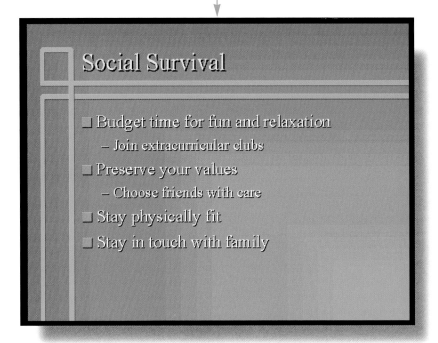

FIGURE 1-46

Displaying the Popup Menu in Slide Show View

Slide Show view has a shortcut menu, called **Popup Menu**, that displays when you right-click a slide in Slide Show view. The Popup Menu contains commands to assist you during a slide show. For example, clicking the **Next command** moves you to the next slide. Clicking the **Previous command** moves you to the previous slide. You can jump to any slide in your presentation by clicking the **Go To command**, which displays the Slide Navigator dialog box. The Slide Navigator dialog box contains a list of the slides in your presentation. Jump to the requested slide by double-clicking the name of that slide.

Additional Popup Menu commands allow you to create a list of action items during a slide show, change the mouse pointer from an arrow to a pen, blacken the screen, and end the slide show. Popup Menu commands are discussed in subsequent projects. Perform the step on the next page to display the Slide Show View Popup Menu.

> **Other Ways**
>
> 1. Press PAGE DOWN to advance one slide at a time, or press PAGE UP to go backward one slide at a time

> **More** *About*
> **Slide Show View**
>
> The Pen command on the Popup Menu turns the mouse pointer into a pen that you can use to mark on the slides. The effect is similar to the electronic white board used by television sports announcers as they explain a play. The markings are not saved with the presentation.

Steps **To Display the Slide Show View Popup Menu**

1 **With Slide 4 displaying in Slide Show view, right-click the slide.**

The Popup menu displays on Slide 4 (Figure 1-47). Your screen may look different because the Popup menu displays near the location of the mouse pointer at the time you right-click.

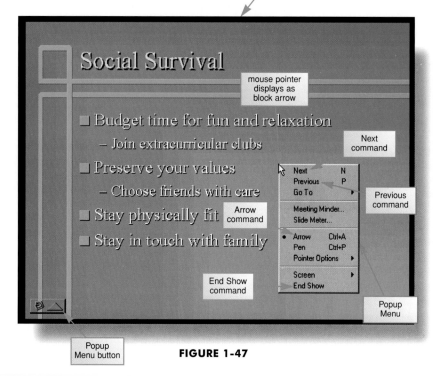

FIGURE 1-47

OtherWays

1. Move mouse pointer during slide show to display the Popup Menu button, then click Popup Menu button

Some presenters prefer to right-click to move backward through a slide show. Because you can display the Slide Show view Popup menu by clicking the Slide Show view Popup Menu button, you can turn off an option setting that displays the Slide Navigator when you right-click. To turn off the Popup Menu on the Right Mouse Click, on the Tools menu, click Options, click the View tab to display the View sheet, click Popup Menu on Right Mouse Click, and then click the OK button. After turning off the Popup Menu on the Right Mouse Click option setting, you can right-click to move backward, one slide at a time, in Slide Show view.

Using the Popup Menu to End a Slide Show

The **End Show command** on the Popup Menu exits Slide Show view and returns to the view you were in when you clicked the Slide Show button. Perform the following step to end Slide Show view.

To Use the Popup Menu to End a Slide Show

1 **Click End Show on the Popup Menu.**

PowerPoint exits Slide Show view and displays the slide last displayed in Slide Show view, which in this instance, is Slide 4 (Figure 1-48).

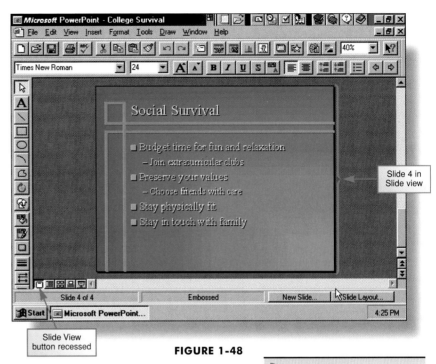

FIGURE 1-48

Other Ways

1. Click the last slide in presentation to return to the slide at which you began Slide Show view
2. Press ESC to display slide last viewed in Slide Show view

Slide Show view is excellent for rehearsing a presentation. You can start Slide Show view from any view: Slide view, Outline view, Slide Sorter view, or Notes Pages view.

Closing PowerPoint

The College Survival presentation now is complete. When you close PowerPoint, PowerPoint prompts you to save any changes made to the presentation since the last save, closes all PowerPoint windows, and then quits PowerPoint. Closing PowerPoint returns control to the desktop. Perform the steps on the next page to close PowerPoint.

Steps **To Close PowerPoint**

1 **Point to the Close button on the title bar (Figure 1-49).**

2 **Click the Close button.**

If you made changes to the presentation since your last save, the Microsoft PowerPoint dialog box displays asking the question, Save changes to "College Survival"?. Click the Yes button to save the changes to the College Survival presentation before closing PowerPoint. Click the No button to close PowerPoint without saving the changes to the College Survival presentation. Click the Cancel button to terminate the Close command and return to the presentation. If you did not make changes to your presentation since your last save, this dialog box does not display.

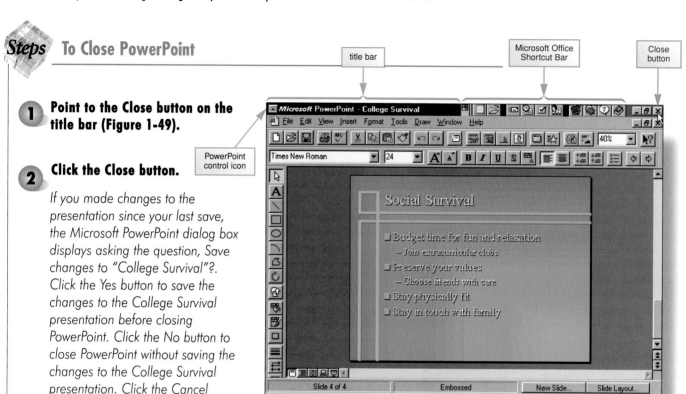

FIGURE 1-49

Opening a Presentation

Earlier, you saved the presentation on a floppy disk using the filename, College Survival.ppt. Once you create and save a presentation, you may need to retrieve it from the floppy disk to make changes. For example, you may want to replace the Design Template or modify some text. Recall that a presentation is a PowerPoint document. Use the **Open Office Document command** to open an existing presentation.

Opening an Existing Presentation

Ensure that the data floppy disk used to save College Survival.ppt is in drive A. Then perform the following steps to open the College Survival presentation using the Open Office Document command on the Start menu.

Steps To Open an Existing Presentation

1 **Click the Start button on the taskbar and point to Open Office Document.**

The Windows 95 Start menu displays (Figure 1-50). Open Office Document is highlighted.

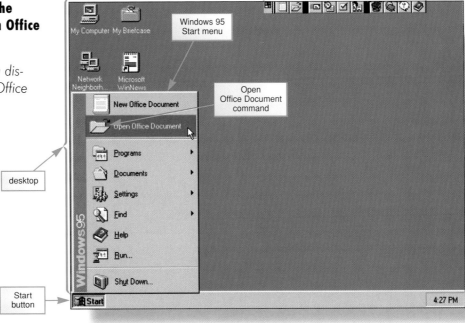

FIGURE 1-50

2 **Click Open Office Document. When the Open dialog box displays, click the Look in box arrow and then click 3½ Floppy [A:] (see Figures 1-21 and 1-22 on page PP 1.23 to review this process).**

The Open dialog box displays (Figure 1-51). A list of existing files on drive A displays because your data floppy disk is in drive A. Notice that Office Files displays in the Files of type drop-down list box. The file, College Survival, is highlighted. Your list of existing files may be different depending on the files saved on your data floppy disk.

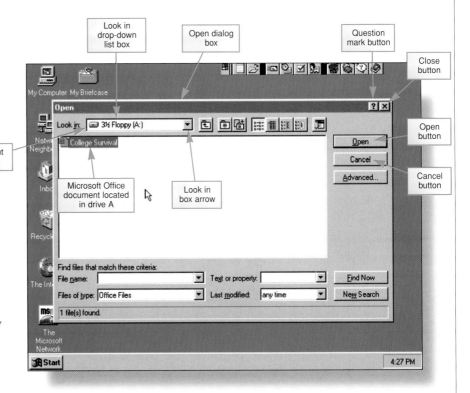

FIGURE 1-51

3 **Double-click College Survival.**

PowerPoint starts and opens College Survival.ppt from drive A into main memory and displays the first slide on the screen (Figure 1-52). The presentation displays in Slide view because PowerPoint opens presentations in the same view in which they were saved.

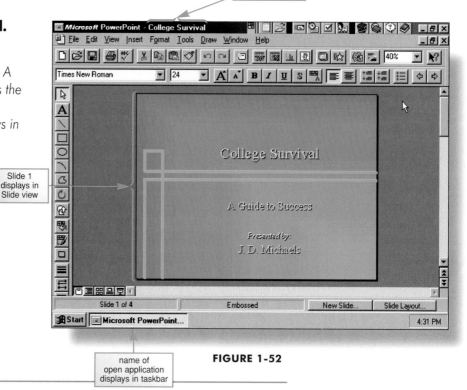

FIGURE 1-52

OtherWays

1. Click Open a Document button on Microsoft Office Shortcut Bar, click folder or drive name in Look in drop-down list box, double-click document name

2. On Start menu click Documents, click document name

When an application is open, its name displays on a button on the taskbar. The **active application** is the one displaying in the foreground of the desktop. That application's corresponding button on the taskbar appears recessed.

When more than one application is open, you can switch between applications by clicking the button labeled with the name of the application to which you want to switch.

Checking a Presentation for Visual Clarity, Consistency, and Style

After you create a presentation, you should proofread it for errors. Typical errors include spelling errors, punctuation errors, and design errors. PowerPoint has a tool, called **Style Checker**, that helps you identify errors in your presentation. When you start Style Checker, the Style Checker dialog box displays three check boxes: Spelling, Visual Clarity, and Case and End Punctuation. A check mark in a check box instructs Style Checker to look for that particular type of inconsistency. For example, a check mark in the Spelling check box causes Style Checker to check the presentation for spelling errors. Table 1-3 identifies the purpose of each check box in the Style Checker dialog box.

Table 1-3	
CHECK BOX	**PURPOSE**
Spelling	Checks the presentation for spelling errors.
Visual Clarity	Checks the presentation for design and style errors, such as fonts too small for the audience to read, too many bullets on a slide, or too many words per paragraph.
Case and End Punctuation	Checks the presentation for consistent usage of capitalization and end punctuation.

PowerPoint checks your presentation for spelling errors using a standard dictionary contained in the Microsoft Office group. This dictionary is shared with the other Microsoft Office applications such as Word and Excel. A **custom dictionary** is available if you want to add special words such as proper names, cities, and acronyms. When checking a presentation for spelling errors, PowerPoint opens the standard dictionary and the custom dictionary file, if one exists. If a word is not found in either dictionary, PowerPoint displays a dialog box. When a word appears in the Spelling dialog box, you have several options which are explained in Table 1-4.

Table 1-4

OPTION	DESCRIPTION
Manually correct the word	Retype the word with the proper spelling and click Change. PowerPoint continues checking the rest of the presentation.
Ignore the word	Click Ignore when the word is spelled correctly but not found in the dictionaries. PowerPoint continues checking the rest of the presentation.
Ignore all occurrences of the word	Click Ignore All when the word is spelled correctly but not found in the dictionaries. PowerPoint ignores all occurrences of the word and continues checking the rest of the presentation.
Select a different spelling	Click the proper spelling of the word from the list in the Suggestions box. Click Change. PowerPoint corrects the word and continues checking the rest of the presentation.
Change all occurrences of the misspelling to a different spelling	Click the proper spelling of the word on the list in the Suggestions box. Click Change All. PowerPoint changes all occurrences of the misspelled word and continues checking the rest of the presentation.
Add a word to the custom dictionary	Click Add. PowerPoint opens the custom dictionary, adds the word, and continues checking the rest of the presentation.
Suggest alternative spellings	Click Suggest. PowerPoint lists suggested spellings. Click the correct word from the Suggestions box or type the proper spelling. Then Click Change. PowerPoint continues checking the rest of the presentation.

The standard dictionary contains commonly used English words. It does not, however, contain proper names, abbreviations, technical terms, poetic contractions, or antiquated terms. PowerPoint treats words not found in the dictionaries as misspellings.

Starting Style Checker

Start Style Checker by clicking the Style Checker command on the Tools menu. Perform the steps on the next pages to start Style Checker.

More *About* **Presentation Design**

Keep to one concept per slide. Highlight the subject rather than presenting a page of text. Limit your slide to five to seven words per line and five to seven lines per slide. Do not clutter; use empty space effectively.

Steps To Start Style Checker

1 **Click Tools on the menu bar. Then point to Style Checker (Figure 1-53).**

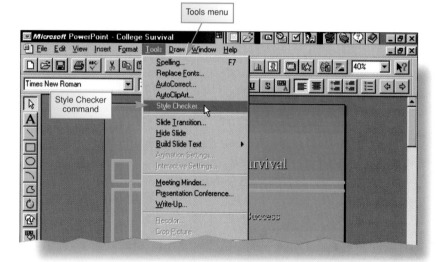

FIGURE 1-53

2 **Click Style Checker. When the Style Checker dialog box displays, point to the Start button.**

The Style Checker dialog box displays (Figure 1-54). A check mark displays in each of the three check boxes in the Check For box. The mouse pointer points to the Start button.

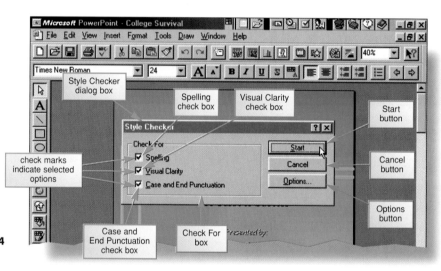

FIGURE 1-54

3 **Click the Start button.**

PowerPoint launches the spelling feature and displays the Spelling dialog box (Figure 1-55). Michaels displays in the Not in Dictionary box. Because it is a common proper name, two suggested spellings display in the Suggestions box. PowerPoint suggests that Michaels should be the possessive form, Michael's, and displays the suggested spelling in the Change To box.

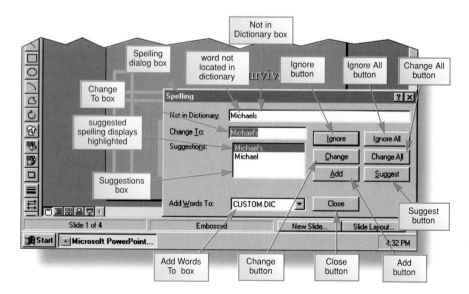

FIGURE 1-55

4 Click the Ignore button.

PowerPoint ignores the word Michaels and continues searching for additional misspelled words. PowerPoint may stop on additional words depending on your typing accuracy. When PowerPoint has checked all slides for misspellings, it begins checking for style errors and displays the Style Checker dialog box (Figure 1-56). The Style Checker dialog box displays a message indicating the slide number currently being checked and displays punctuation errors. If you have punctuation errors, you can click one of the buttons to ignore or change them. If you want to stop Style Checker and return to the current slide, click the Cancel button.

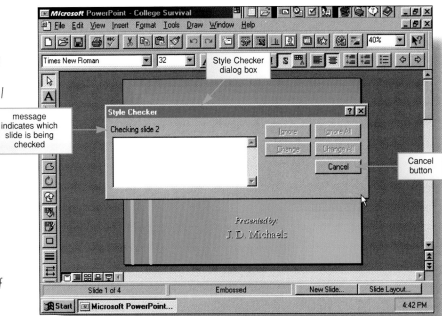

FIGURE 1-56

5 If the Style Checker lists visual clarity inconsistencies in the Style Checker Summary dialog box, write the slide number and the message on a sheet of paper (Figure 1-57).

6 Click the OK button.

PowerPoint closes Style Checker and returns to the current slide, Slide 1, or to the slide where a misspelled word occurred.

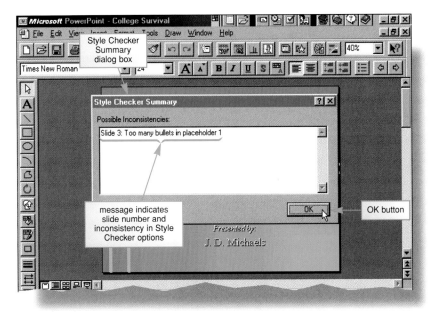

FIGURE 1-57

The Style Checker dialog box contains an **Options button** (see Figure 1-54), which when clicked, displays the Style Checker Options dialog box. The Style Checker Options dialog box has two tabbed sheets: Case and End Punctuation, and Visual Clarity. Each tabbed sheet has several options that can be changed to suit your design specifications. Table 1-5 on the next page identifies each option available in Style Checker and each default setting.

Table 1-5	
OPTION	*SETTING*
CASE	
Slide Title Style	Title Case
Body Text Style	Sentence Case
END PUNCTUATION	
Slide Title Periods	Remove
Body Text Periods	Remove
VISUAL CLARITY	
Number of Fonts Should Not Exceed	3
Title	36 points
Body Text Size Should Be at Least	24 points
Number of Bullets Should Be at Least	6
Number of Lines per Title Should Be at Least	2
Number of Lines per Bullet Should Be at Least	2
Check for Title and Placeholder Text Off Slide	On

Correcting Errors

After creating a presentation and running Style Checker, you may find that you must make changes. Changes may be required because a slide contains an error, the scope of the presentation shifts, or Style Checker found a style inconsistency. This section explains the types of errors that commonly occur when creating a presentation.

Types of Corrections Made to Presentations

There usually are three types of corrections to text in a presentation: additions, deletions, and replacements.

▶ **Additions** — Additions are necessary when you omit text from a slide and need to add it later. You may need to insert text in the form of a sentence, word, or single character. For example, you may want to add the rest of the presenter's first name on your title slide.

▶ **Deletions** — Deletions are required when text on a slide is incorrect or is no longer relevant to the presentation. For example, Style Checker identified too many bullets on Slide 3. Therefore, you may want to remove one of the bulleted paragraphs.

▶ **Replacements** — Replacements are needed when you want to revise the text in your presentation. For example, you may want to substitute the word their for the word there.

Editing text in PowerPoint is basically the same as editing text in a word processing package. The following sections illustrate the most common changes made to text in a presentation.

Deleting Text

There are three methods for deleting text. One is to use the BACKSPACE key to remove text just typed. The second is to position the insertion point to the left of the text you wish to delete and then press the DELETE key. The third method is to drag through the text you wish to delete and press the DELETE key. (Use the third method when deleting large sections of text.)

Previously, Style Checker identified that Slide 3 has too many bullets. Perform the following steps to delete one of the bulleted paragraphs.

TO DELETE A PARAGRAPH

Step 1: Drag the elevator to display Slide 3.
Step 2: Click the bullet in front of the first paragraph, Learn your way around campus.
Step 3: Press the DELETE key.

The selected paragraph is deleted from Slide 3. The remaining 6 bulleted paragraphs move up one paragraph in the text object to take the place of the deleted paragraph. Slide 3 now satisfies the Style Checker design rule, not to exceed 6 bullets per slide.

Recall from the beginning of this project that if you make a mistake (such as deleting text), you can click the Undo button on the Standard toolbar to reverse your mistake.

OtherWays

1. On Edit menu click Clear

Replacing Text into an Existing Slide

When you need to correct a word or phrase, you can replace the text by selecting the text to be replaced and then typing the new text. As soon as you press any key on the keyboard, the highlighted text is deleted and the new text displays.

PowerPoint inserts text to the left of the insertion point. The text to the right of the insertion point moves to the right (and shifts downward if necessary) to accommodate the added text. Perform the following steps to replace the period after the letter J with the rest of J. D. Michaels' first name, Jerry.

TO REPLACE TEXT

Step 1: Drag the elevator to display Slide 1. Select the period between the J and the D in J. D. Michaels by dragging the I-beam mouse pointer.

Step 2: Type erry to replace the period and insert the rest of the first name, Jerry.

The title slide now displays Jerry D. Michaels first name, as shown in Figure 1-2 on page PP 1.9, instead of his initials.

Changing Line Spacing

The bulleted lists on Slides 2, 3, and 4 look crowded; yet, there is ample blank space that could be used to separate the paragraphs. You can adjust the spacing on each slide, but when several slides need to be changed, you should change the Slide Master. Each PowerPoint component (slides, audience handouts, and notes pages) has a **master**, which controls its appearance. Slides have two masters, Title Master and Slide Master. The **Title Master** controls the appearance of the title slide. The **Slide Master** controls the appearance of the other slides in your presentation.

Each Design Template has a specially designed Slide Master; so if you select a Design Template, but want to change one of its components, you can override that component by changing the Slide Master. Any change to the Slide Master results in changing every slide in the presentation, except the title slide. For example, if you change the line spacing to .5 inches before each paragraph on the Slide Master, each slide (except the title slide) changes line spacing after each paragraph to .5 inches. The Slide Master components most frequently changed are listed in Table 1-6.

Table 1-6	
COMPONENT	DESCRIPTION
Font face	Defines the appearance and shape of letters, numbers, and special characters.
Font size	Specifies the size of the characters on the screen. Character size is gauged by a measurement system called points. A single point is about 1/72 of an inch in height. Thus, a character with a point size of eighteen is about 18/72 (or 1/4) of an inch in height.
Text style	Text styles include plain, italic, bold, shadowed, and underlined. Text may have more than one style at a time.
Text position	Positions of text in a paragraph left aligned, right aligned, centered, or justified. Justified text is proportionally spaced across the object.
Color scheme	A coordinated set of eight colors designed to complement each other. Color schemes consist of background color, line and text color, shadow color, title text color, object fill color, and three different accent colors.
Background items	Any object other than the title object or text object. Typical items include borders, graphics—such as a company logo, page number, date, and time.
Slide number	Inserts the special symbol used to print the slide number.
Date	Inserts the special symbol used to print the date the presentation was printed.
Time	Inserts the special symbol used to print the time the presentation was printed.

Additionally, each view has its own master. You can access the master by holding down the SHIFT key while clicking the appropriate view button. For example, holding down the SHIFT key and clicking the Slide view button displays the Slide Master. To exit a master, click the view button to which you wish to return. To return to Slide view, for example, click the Slide View button.

Displaying the Slide Master

Before you can change line spacing on the Slide Master, you first must display it. Perform the following steps to display the Slide Master.

Steps **To Display the Slide Master**

1 **Drag the elevator to display Slide 2. Press and hold down the SHIFT key and then point to the Slide View button.**

When you hold down the SHIFT key, the ToolTip box displays Slide Master (Figure 1-58).

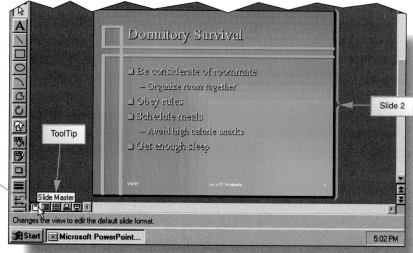

FIGURE 1-58

2 **While holding down the SHIFT key, click the Slide View button. Then release the SHIFT key.**

The Slide Master displays (Figure 1-59).

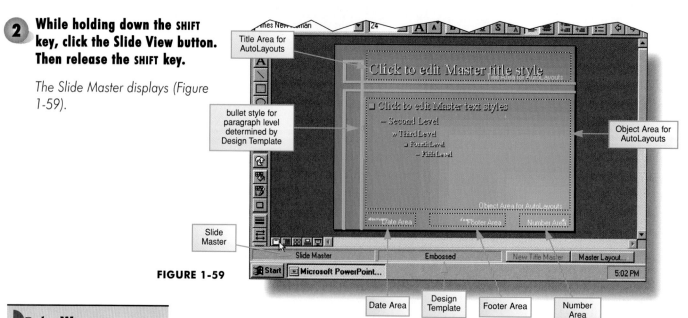

FIGURE 1-59

Other Ways

1. On View menu click Master, click Slide Master

Changing Line Spacing on the Slide Master

Change line spacing by clicking the Line Spacing command on the Format menu. When you click the **Line Spacing command**, the Line Spacing dialog box displays. The Line Spacing dialog box contains three boxes, Line Spacing, Before Paragraph, and After Paragraph, which allow you to adjust line spacing within a paragraph, before a paragraph, and after a paragraph, respectively.

In this project, you change the number in the amount of space box to increase the amount of space that displays before every paragraph, except the first paragraph, on every slide. For example, increasing the amount of space box to 0.5 lines increases the amount of space that displays before each paragraph. The first paragraph on every slide, however, does not change. Perform the following steps to change the line spacing.

 Steps **To Change Line Spacing on the Slide Master**

1 **Click the bulleted paragraph labeled, Click to edit Master text styles.**

The insertion point displays at the point you clicked (Figure 1-60). The text object area is selected.

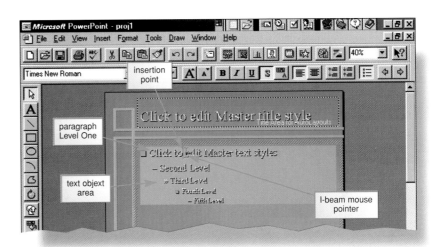

FIGURE 1-60

2 **Click Format on the menu bar and then point to Line Spacing (Figure 1-61).**

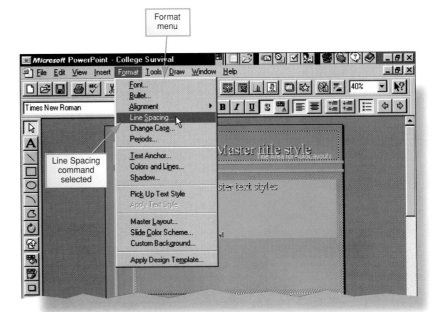

FIGURE 1-61

3 Click Line Spacing. Point to the up arrow in the amount of space box in the Before Paragraph box.

PowerPoint displays the Line Spacing dialog box (Figure 1-62).

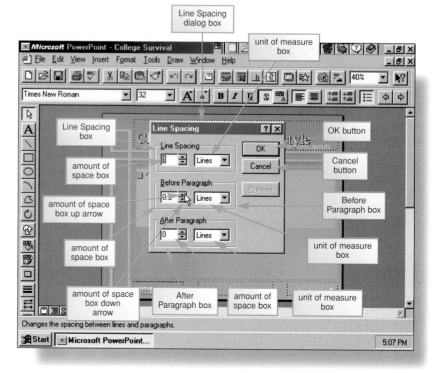

FIGURE 1-62

4 Click the amount of space box up arrow six times so that 0.5 displays.

The amount of space box displays 0.5 (Figure 1-63). The Preview button is available after a change is made in the Line Spacing dialog box.

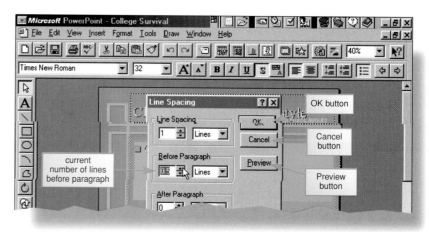

FIGURE 1-63

5 Click the OK button.

The Slide Master text placeholder displays the new Before Paragraph line spacing (Figure 1-64). Depending on the video drivers installed, the spacing on your screen may appear slightly different than this figure.

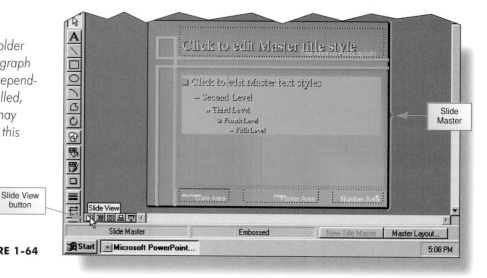

FIGURE 1-64

6 **Click the Slide View button to return to Slide view.**

Slide 2 displays with the Before Paragraph line spacing set to 0.5 lines (Figure 1-65).

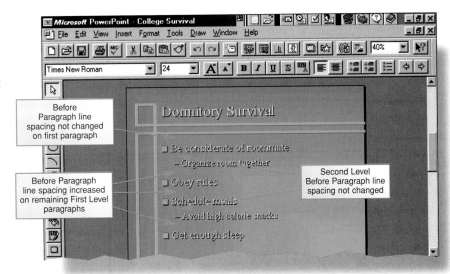

FIGURE 1-65

To display your line spacing changes without making them permanent, click the Preview button. If you want to close the Line Spacing dialog box without applying the changes, click the Cancel button.

Before Paragraph line spacing is controlled by setting the number of units before a paragraph. Units are either lines or points; lines are the default unit. Points may be selected by clicking the down arrow next to the Before Paragraph drop-down list box (see Figure 1-62). Recall from page PP 1.19 that a single point is about 1/72 of an inch in height.

The Line Spacing box and the After Paragraph box each contain an amount of space box and a unit of measure box. To change the amount of space displaying between paragraphs, click the amount of space box up arrow or down arrow in the Line Spacing box. To change the amount of space displaying after a paragraph, click the amount of space box up arrow or down arrow in the After Paragraph box. To change the unit of measure from Lines to Points in either the Line Spacing box or the After Paragraph box, click the down arrow next to the unit of measure drop-down list box and then click Points.

The placeholder at the top of the Slide Master (Figure 1-64) is used to edit the Master title style. The large placeholder under the Master title placeholder is used to edit the Master text styles. Here you make changes to the various bullet levels. Changes can be made to line spacing, bullet font, text and line color, alignment, and text shadow. It is also the object area for AutoLayouts.

More *About* **Line Spacing**

Resist the temptation to regard blank space on a slide as wasted space. Blank space added for the purpose of directing the attention of the audience to specific text or graphics is called **white space**. White space is a powerful design tool. Used effectively, white space improves audience attention.

Displaying a Presentation in Black and White

This project explains how to print a presentation for the purpose of making transparencies. PowerPoint's **B&W View button** allows you to display the presentation in black and white before you print it. Table 1-7 identifies how PowerPoint objects display in black and white.

Table 1-7	
OBJECT	**APPEARANCE IN BLACK AND WHITE VIEW**
Text	Black
Text shadows	Hidden
Embossing	Hidden
Fills	Grayscale
Frame	1 point frame
Pattern fills	Grayscale
Lines	Black
Object shadows	Gray
Bitmaps/Pictures	Grayscale
Slide backgrounds	White

Perform the following steps to display the presentation in black and white.

Steps   To Display a Presentation in Black and White

1 **Point to the B&W View button on the Standard toolbar (Figure 1-66).**

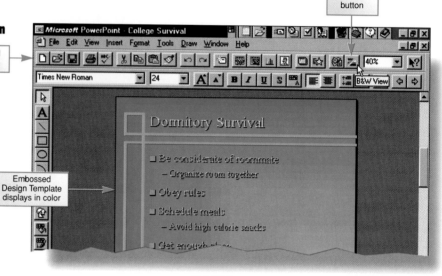

FIGURE 1-66

2 **Click the B&W View button.**

The presentation displays in black and white (Figure 1-67). The B&W View button is recessed. The Color View box displays a miniature of the current slide in color.

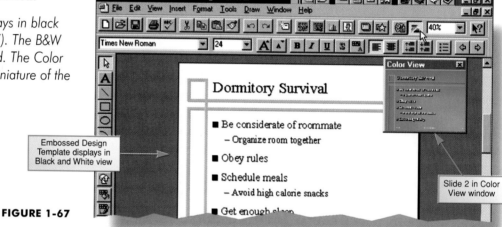

FIGURE 1-67

OtherWays

1. On View menu click Black and White

To return to the color view of the presentation, click the B&W View button again.

Printing a Presentation

After you create a presentation, you often want to print it. A printed version of the presentation is called a **hard copy**, or **printout**. The first printing of the presentation is called a **rough draft**. The rough draft allows you to proofread the presentation to check for errors and readability. After correcting errors, you print the final copy of your presentation.

Saving Before Printing

Prior to printing your presentation, you should save your work in the event you experience difficulties with the printer. You occasionally may encounter system problems that can be resolved only by restarting the computer. In such an instance, you will need to reopen your presentation. As a precaution, always save your presentation before you print. Perform the following steps to save the presentation before printing.

TO SAVE A PRESENTATION BEFORE PRINTING

Step 1: Verify that your data floppy disk is in drive A.
Step 2: Click the Save button on the Standard toolbar.

All changes made after your last save are now saved on a floppy disk.

Printing the Presentation

After saving the presentation, you are ready to print. Because you are in Slide view, clicking the **Print button** on the Standard toolbar causes PowerPoint to print all slides in the presentation. Additionally, because you are currently viewing the presentation in black and white, the slides print in black and white, even if you have a color printer. Perform the following steps to print the presentation slides.

 Steps To Print a Presentation

1 **Ready the printer according to the printer instructions. Then, click the Print button on the Standard toolbar.**

The mouse pointer momentarily changes to an hourglass. PowerPoint then displays a message on the status bar indicating it is preparing to print the presentation in the background. An animated printer icon displays on the status bar identifying which slide is being prepared. After several moments, the presentation begins printing on the printer. The printer icon, next to the clock on the taskbar, indicates there is a print job processing (Figure 1-68). When the presentation is finished printing, the printer icon on the taskbar disappears.

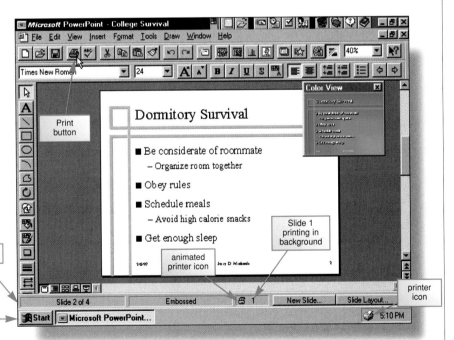

FIGURE 1-68

2 **When the printer stops, retrieve the printouts of the slides.**

The presentation, College Survival, prints on four pages (Figure 1-69).

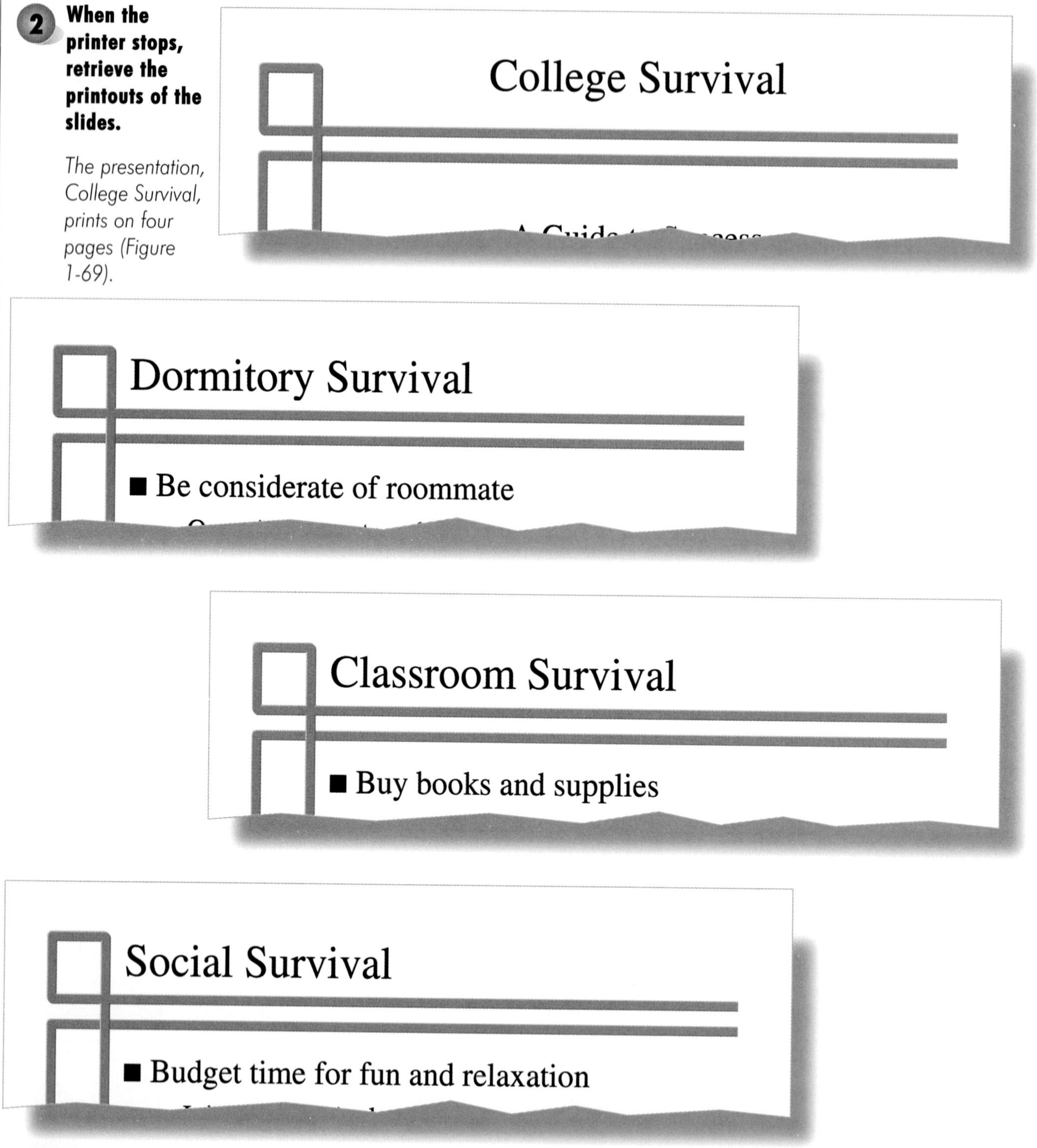

College Survival

A Guide to Success

Dormitory Survival

■ Be considerate of roommate

Classroom Survival

■ Buy books and supplies

Social Survival

■ Budget time for fun and relaxation

FIGURE 1-69

OtherWays
1. On File menu click Print
2. Press CTRL+P, or press CTRL+SHIFT+F12

Double-clicking the animated printer icon on the status bar cancels the printing process.

Making a Transparency

This project requires you to make overhead transparencies. You make transparencies using one of several devices. One device is a printer attached to your computer, such as an ink jet printer or a laser printer. Transparencies produced on a printer may be in black and white or color, depending on the printer. Another device is a photocopier. A third device is a thermal copier. A thermal copier transfers a carbonaceous substance, like toner from a photocopier, from a paper master to an acetate film. Because each of the three devices requires a special transparency film, check the user's manual for the film requirement of your specific device, or ask your instructor.

PowerPoint Help

You can get assistance anytime while you are working in PowerPoint using **online help**. When used effectively, online help can increase your productivity and reduce the amount of time you spend learning how to use PowerPoint. Table 1-8 summarizes the six categories of online help.

The following sections show examples of each category of online help described in Table 1-8.

Using the Contents Sheet to Obtain Help

The **Contents sheet** in the Help Topics dialog box assists you in finding help about a specific subject. Use the Contents sheet in the same manner you use the table of contents in a book. Perform the steps on the next page to use the Contents sheet to obtain help on using the Slide Master to change the appearance of your presentation.

Table 1-8

HELP CATEGORY	SUMMARY	HOW TO START
Answer Wizard sheet	Allows you to enter, in your own words, an English-type question. For example, How do I change bullet fonts?	Double-click the Help button on the Standard toolbar; or on the Help menu, click Microsoft PowerPoint Help Topics, and then click the Answer Wizard tab.
Contents sheet	Groups help topics by general categories. Use when you know, in general, what you want.	Double-click the Help button on the Standard toolbar; or on the Help menu, click Microsoft PowerPoint Help Topics, and then click the Contents tab.
Find sheet	Searches the index for all phrases that include the term you specify. For example, bullets.	Double-click the Help button on the Standard toolbar; or on the Help menu, click Microsoft PowerPoint Help Topics, and then click the Find tab.
Help button	Provides an explanation of objects on the screen.	Click the Help button on the Standard toolbar and then click an object on the screen.
Index sheet	Lists help topics alphabetically. Similar to an index in a book. Use when you know exactly what you want. For example, adding footers.	Double-click the Help button on the Standard toolbar; or on the Help menu, click Microsoft PowerPoint Help Topics, and then click the Index tab.
Question mark button	Provides an explanation of objects on the screen.	In a dialog box, click the Question mark button and then click a dialog box object.

Steps To Obtain Help Using the Contents Sheet

1 **Double-click the Help button on the Standard toolbar.**

The Help Topics: Microsoft PowerPoint dialog box displays.

2 **If necessary, click the Contents tab to activate the Contents sheet. In the list box, double-click the book icon labeled Changing the Appearance of Your Presentation.**

*An icon precedes each entry in the list box. A **Book icon** indicates there are subtopics. A **Question mark icon** indicates information will display when the title is double-clicked (Figure 1-70).*

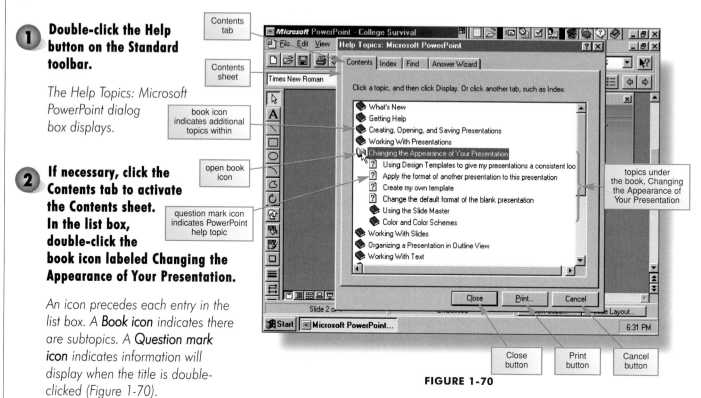

FIGURE 1-70

3 **Double-click the topic labeled Using Design Templates to give my presentations a consistent look.**

A Microsoft PowerPoint window displays information about using Design Templates to give a presentation a consistent look (Figure 1-71).

4 **After reading the information, click the Close button in the Microsoft PowerPoint window.**

The Microsoft PowerPoint window closes.

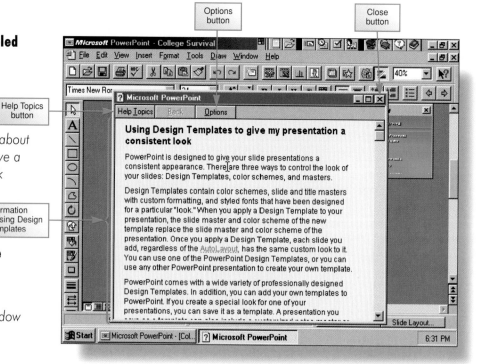

FIGURE 1-71

OtherWays

1. On Help menu click Microsoft PowerPoint Help Topics, click Contents tab
2. Press F1

As an alternative to double-clicking the topic name in the list box, you can click it and then use the buttons at the bottom of the Microsoft PowerPoint window to display information on a topic or print information on a topic (Figure 1-70). Additionally, you can print information on a topic by pointing to the help window, right-clicking, and then clicking Print Topic; or by clicking the Options button at the top of the Microsoft PowerPoint window, and then clicking Print Topic (Figure 1-71). To close or cancel the Microsoft PowerPoint window, click the Close button to return to PowerPoint, or click the **Help Topics button** to return to the Contents sheet.

Using the Index Sheet to Obtain Help

Use the **Index sheet** in the Help Topics: Microsoft PowerPoint dialog box when you know the term about which you are seeking help. You can locate the term you are looking for by typing part or all of the word, or you can scroll through the alphabetical list and click the term. You use the Index sheet in the same manner you use an index at the back of a book.

Many of the online help topics provide you with a demonstration of how to accomplish a task. For example, if you want to find out how to add footers to the Slide Master, PowerPoint shows you by pointing to the View menu and then pointing to the Header and Footer command. Perform the following steps to obtain information about adding footers to the Slide Master by typing foo, the first three letters of the word footer.

Steps **To Obtain Help Using the Index Sheet**

1 **Double-click the Help button on the Standard toolbar.**

The Help Topics: Microsoft PowerPoint dialog box displays.

2 **If necessary, click the Index tab to display the Index sheet. Type** foo **in the box labeled 1.**

The term footers is highlighted in the box labeled 2 (Figure 1-72).

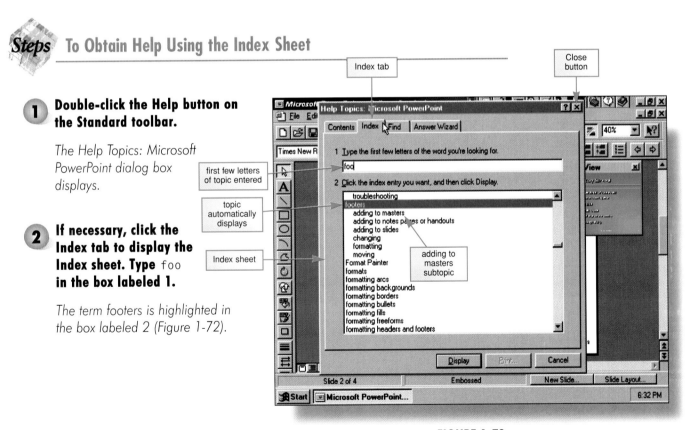

FIGURE 1-72

3 Double-click the subtopic labeled adding to masters (see Figure 1-72 on the previous page).

PowerPoint demonstrates how to add footers to the Slide Master. After which, PowerPoint displays a ScreenTip about the Slide Master (Figure 1-73).

4 After reading the information, click anywhere outside the ScreenTip to close it.

The ScreenTip closes.

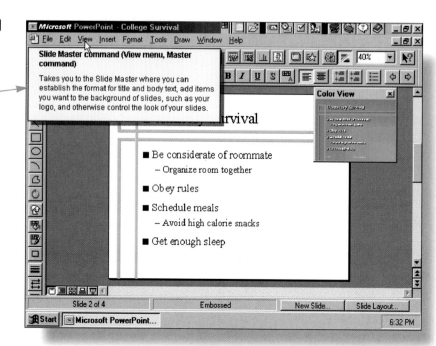

FIGURE 1-73

OtherWays

1. On Help menu click Microsoft PowerPoint Help Topics, click Index tab
2. Press F1

More *About* **Presentation Design**

Two acronyms pertain directly to presentation design:
— K.I.S. (Keep It Simple)
— C.C.C. (Clutter Creates Confusion)

Not all online help information is printable. For example, the Slide Master ScreenTip (Figure 1-73) is not printable. Generally speaking, if the window contains an Options button (Figure 1-71 on page PP 1.54), you can print the information.

Using the Find Sheet to Obtain Help

The **Find sheet** in the Help Topics: Microsoft PowerPoint dialog box locates the word or phrase you want. Use the Find sheet when you wish to find information about a term or a word contained within a phrase. The Find sheet displays a list of all topics pertaining to the specified term or phrase. You then can narrow your search by selecting words or phrases from the list. Perform the following steps to obtain information about changing the distance between bullets and text.

Steps To Obtain Help Using the Find Sheet

1 **Double-click the Help button on the Standard toolbar.**

The Help Topics: Microsoft PowerPoint dialog box displays.

2 **If necessary, click the Find tab. Type** bulleted **in the box labeled 1. Then point to the topic in the box labeled 3, change the distance between bullets and text.**

Three topics display in the box labeled 3 that contain the word bulleted. The topic, Add, change, or remove a bullet, is highlighted (Figure 1-74).

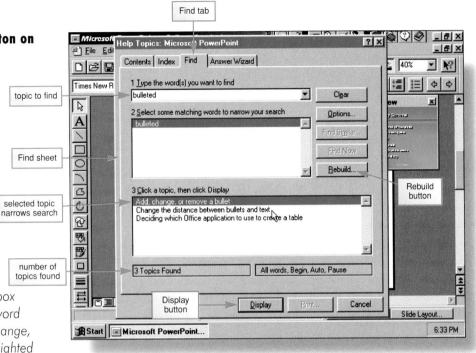

FIGURE 1-74

3 **Double-click the topic, Change the distance between bullets and text, in the box labeled 3 on the Find sheet. When the Microsoft PowerPoint window displays the information about changing the distance between bullets and text, point to the green underlined words, slide master, located in the Note at the bottom of the Microsoft PowerPoint window.**

A Microsoft PowerPoint window displays information about changing the distance between bullets and text. The green underlined text at the bottom of the Microsoft PowerPoint window identifies a jump to additional information (Figure 1-75a).

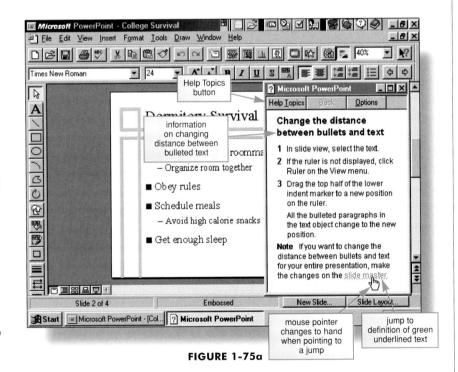

FIGURE 1-75a

4 **Click slide master.**

Clicking the green underlined text displays a ScreenTip (Figure 1-75b). The ScreenTip provides additional information about the word (often a definition).

5 **Read the ScreenTip, and then click the Close button on the Microsoft PowerPoint window two times.**

Clicking the Close button once closes the ScreenTip. Clicking the Close button a second time closes the Microsoft PowerPoint window and returns to PowerPoint.

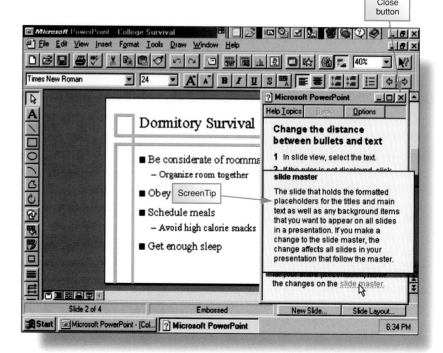

FIGURE 1-75b

OtherWays

1. On Help menu click Microsoft PowerPoint Help Topics, click Find tab
2. Press F1

You may specify more than one word in the box labeled 1 (Figure 1-74 on the previous page) if you separate the words with a space. If you specify words in uppercase letters, then only uppercase occurrences of the words (within the Help Topics) are found. If you specify words in lowercase letters, however, both uppercase and lowercase occurrences of the words are found. Search options can be changed by clicking the Options button on the Find sheet.

Using the Answer Wizard Sheet to Obtain Help

The last sheet in the Help Topics: Microsoft PowerPoint dialog box is the Answer Wizard sheet. Use the **Answer Wizard sheet** when you know what you want to do but do not know what the task is called. Recall that the Answer Wizard allows you to ask a question in your own words. The Answer Wizard then finds topics that contain the words in your question. For example, when you type a question such as, What is new? (to find the new features in PowerPoint 95) on the Answer Wizard sheet, it displays two sections: How Do I and Tell Me About. The **How Do I topics** provide you with easy-to-follow instructions. Some step-by-step visual answers take you to the command or option you need to complete the task. The **Tell Me About topics** give you background information about the selected topic.

Perform the following steps to obtain information on the new features in PowerPoint 95 by typing the question, What is new?

Steps To Obtain Help Using the Answer Wizard

1 **Double-click the Help button on the Standard toolbar.**

The Help Topics: Microsoft PowerPoint dialog box displays.

2 **If necessary, click the Answer Wizard tab. Type** What is new? **in the box labeled 1. Click the Search button. Then, in the box labeled 2, in the Tell Me About section, point to the topic, What's new in Microsoft PowerPoint 95.**

The Answer Wizard displays two sections in the box labeled 2: How Do I and Tell Me About (Figure 1-76).

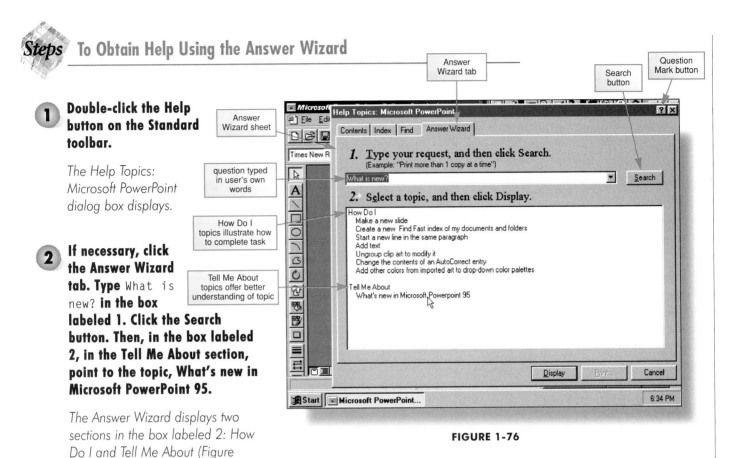

FIGURE 1-76

3 **Double-click What's new in Microsoft PowerPoint 95. Then point to the button in front of AutoCorrect in the Microsoft PowerPoint for Windows 95 window.**

The Microsoft PowerPoint for Windows 95 window displays a list of features new to PowerPoint 95. A button displays in front of each topic. When you point to a topic, the mouse pointer changes to a hand (Figure 1-77).

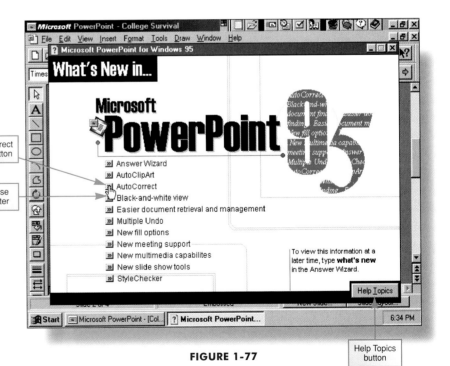

FIGURE 1-77

4 **Click the button in front of AutoCorrect. Click the box labeled Easier to be effective.**

PowerPoint displays a Microsoft PowerPoint for Windows 95 window containing jump boxes that point to specific items on a slide. When you click the jump box labeled Easier to be effective, a ScreenTip displays containing information about AutoCorrect (Figure 1-78).

5 **Read the ScreenTip. Then click the Close button in the Microsoft PowerPoint for Windows 95 window to return to PowerPoint.**

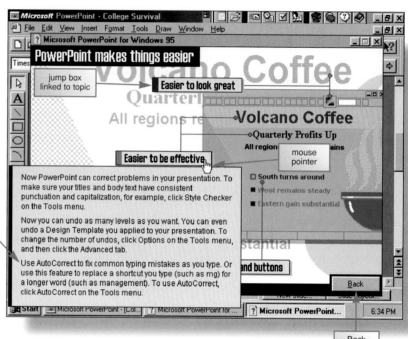

FIGURE 1-78

OtherWays

1. From Help menu click Microsoft PowerPoint Help Topics or Answer Wizard
2. Press F1

As an alternative to clicking the Close button in Step 5, you can click the **Back button** to return to the previous dialog box shown in Figure 1-77 on the previous page.

The four online help features of PowerPoint (Contents, Index, Find, and Answer Wizard) are easy to use, yet powerful. The best way to familiarize yourself with these help tools is to use them. In the Student Assignments at the end of each project is a section titled Use Help. It is recommended that you step through these exercises to gain a better understanding of how PowerPoint online help works.

Using the Help button

When you are not certain about what an object is in the PowerPoint window, use the **Help button**. When you click the Help button, the mouse pointer changes to an arrow with a question mark. Then, when you click an object in the PowerPoint window, a ScreenTip displays. Once you click the Help button, you can move the arrow and question mark pointer to any menu name, button, or object, and click to display a ScreenTip. For example, clicking the Help button, and then clicking the Spelling button on the Standard toolbar results in the ScreenTip shown in Figure 1-79. Click anywhere on the PowerPoint window to close the ScreenTip.

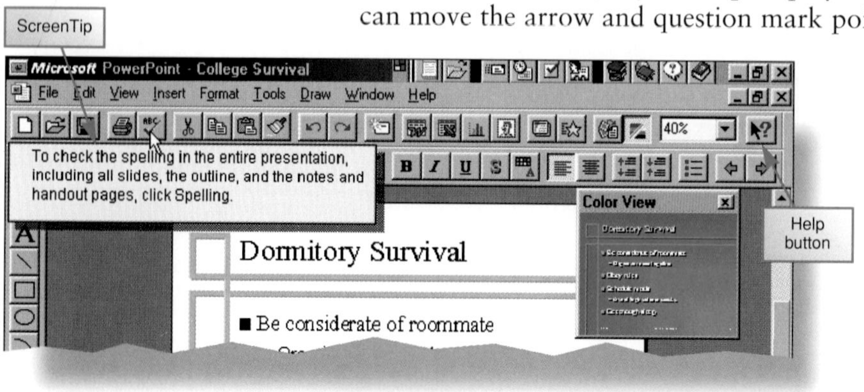

FIGURE 1-79

Using the Question Mark button

The **Question mark button** (see Figure 1-76 on page PP 1.59) is similar to the Help button. Use the Question mark button when you are not certain about the purpose of an object in a dialog box. When you click the Question mark button, the mouse pointer changes to an arrow with a question mark. Then, when you click an object in a dialog box, a ScreenTip displays.

Closing PowerPoint

Project 1 is complete. The final task is to close the presentation and PowerPoint. Perform the following steps to close PowerPoint.

TO CLOSE POWERPOINT

Step 1: Click the Close button on the title bar.
Step 2: Click the Yes button in the Microsoft PowerPoint dialog box.

The Microsoft PowerPoint dialog box displays when you close PowerPoint without first saving any changes (Figure 1-80).

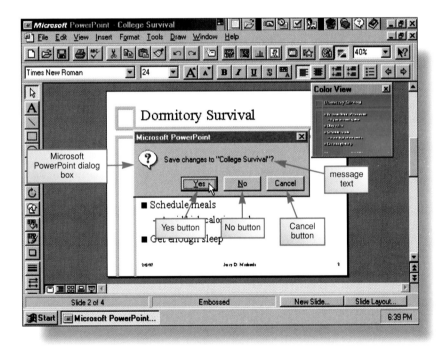

FIGURE 1-80

Clicking the No button in the Microsoft PowerPoint dialog box closes the presentation and PowerPoint without saving the changes made after your last save. Clicking the Cancel button, returns to PowerPoint and the current presentation.

Project Summary

Project 1 introduced you to starting PowerPoint and creating a multi-level bulleted list presentation. You learned about PowerPoint Design Templates, objects, and attributes. Project 1 illustrated how to change the text style to italic and decrease font size on the title slide. Completing these tasks, you saved your presentation. Then, you created three multi-level bulleted list slides. Next, you learned how to view the presentation in Slide Show view. After which, you learned how to close PowerPoint and how to open an existing presentation. Using Style Checker, you learned how to look for spelling errors and identify inconsistencies in design specifications. After running Style Checker, you edited the presentation to correct the design errors and insert text. Using the Slide Master, you adjusted the Before Paragraph line spacing to make better use of white space. You learned how to display the presentation in black and white before printing it; and then, you learned how to print hard copies of your slides. Finally, you learned how to use PowerPoint online help.

What You Should Know

Having completed this project, you now should be able to perform the following tasks:

▶ Add a New Slide with the Bulleted List Auto-Layout *(PP 1.25)*

▶ Add a New Slide with the Same AutoLayout *(PP 1.30)*

▶ Change Line Spacing on the Slide Master *(PP 1.47)*

▶ Change the Style Text to Italic *(PP 1.21)*

▶ Close PowerPoint *(PP 1.38, PP 1.61)*

▶ Decrease Font Size *(PP 1.20)*

▶ Delete a Paragraph *(PP 1.44)*

▶ Display a Presentation in Black and White *(PP 1.50)*

▶ Display the Slide Master *(PP 1.46)*

▶ Display the Slide Show View Popup Menu *(PP 1.36)*

▶ Enter the Presentation Subtitle *(PP 1.18)*

▶ Enter the Presentation Title *(PP 1.17)*

▶ Enter a Slide Title *(PP 1.27)*

▶ Manually Move through Slides in a Slide Show *(PP 1.35)*

▶ Obtain Help Using the Answer Wizard *(PP 1.59)*

▶ Obtain Help Using the Contents Sheet *(PP 1.54)*

▶ Obtain Help Using the Find Sheet *(PP 1.57)*

▶ Obtain Help Using the Index Sheet *(PP 1.55)*

▶ Open an Existing Presentation *(PP 1.38)*

▶ Print a Presentation *(PP 1.51)*

▶ Replace Text *(PP 1.45)*

▶ Save a Presentation to a Floppy Disk *(PP 1.22)*

▶ Save a Presentation with the Same Filename *(PP 1.32, PP 1.51)*

▶ Select a Text Placeholder *(PP 1.27)*

▶ Start a New Presentation *(PP 1.10)*

▶ Start Slide Show View *(PP 1.34)*

▶ Start Style Checker *(PP 1.42)*

▶ Type a Multi-level Bulleted List *(PP 1.28)*

▶ Use the Popup Menu to End a Slide Show *(PP 1.37)*

▶ Use the Vertical Scroll Bar to Move to Another Slide *(PP 1.33)*

A+ Test Your Knowledge

1 True/False

Instructions: Circle T if the statement is true or F if the statement is false.

T F   1. A PowerPoint document is called a presentation.
T F   2. The basic unit of a PowerPoint presentation is a slide.
T F   3. The menu bar displays the name of the current PowerPoint file.
T F   4. Toolbars consist of buttons that access commonly used PowerPoint tools.
T F   5. Objects are the building blocks for a PowerPoint slide.
T F   6. In PowerPoint, the Formatting toolbar contains tools for changing text attributes.
T F   7. Every time you add a slide to an open presentation, PowerPoint prompts you to choose an AutoLayout.
T F   8. PowerPoint assumes the first slide in a presentation is the Slide Master.
T F   9. The function of the Undo button is limited to reversing the last action.
T F   10. The slide indicator shows the slide number and slide title.

2 Multiple Choice

Instructions: Circle the correct response.

1. When the mouse pointer is pointing to a menu, it has the shape of a(n) _____.
   a. hand
   b. hourglass
   c. I-beam
   d. left-pointing block arrow
2. To close a presentation and PowerPoint, click the _____ button.
   a. Save
   b. Save As
   c. Close
   d. Exit
3. _____ displays a single slide in the PowerPoint window as it appears in your presentation.
   a. Slide view
   b. Outline view
   c. Notes Pages view
   d. Slide Sorter view
4. To display online help information by asking a question in your own words, use the _____.
   a. Content sheet
   b. Index sheet
   c. Find sheet
   d. Answer Wizard sheet

(continued)

A+ Test Your Knowledge

Multiple Choice (continued)

5. The Design Template controls the layout and attributes of the _____.
   a. title object
   b. title text
   c. body object
   d. all of the above

6. Before you italicize a paragraph, you must first _____.
   a. highlight the first word in the paragraph to be formatted
   b. highlight the paragraph to be formatted
   c. position the mouse pointer beside the first character in the paragraph to be formatted
   d. underscore the paragraph to be formatted

7. If you add objects to the Slide Master, they display on _____.
   a. the Slide Master
   b. every slide
   c. every slide except the title slide
   d. both a and c

8. To erase a character to the left of the insertion point, press the _____ key.
   a. DELETE
   b. INSERT
   c. BACKSPACE
   d. both a and c

9. When you close PowerPoint, _____.
   a. control is returned to the desktop
   b. the presentation is erased from a floppy disk
   c. the presentation is removed from the screen
   d. both a and c

10. PowerPoint automatically appends the extension _____ to a filename when you save a presentation.
    a. .DOC
    b. .PPT
    c. .TXT
    d. .XLS

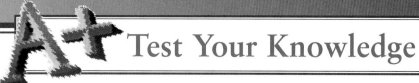

3 Understanding the PowerPoint Window

Instructions: In Figure 1-81, arrows point to the major components of the PowerPoint window. Identify the various parts of the window in the space provided.

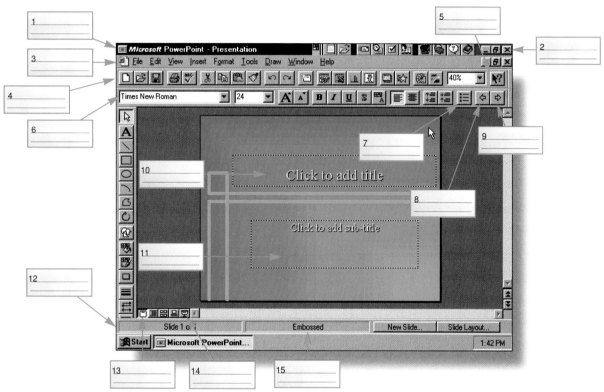

FIGURE 1-81

4 Understanding the PowerPoint Toolbars

Instructions: In Figure 1-82, arrows point to several buttons on the Standard and Formatting toolbars. Identify the buttons in the space provided.

FIGURE 1-82

Use Help

1 Reviewing Project Activities

Instructions: Perform the following tasks using a computer.

1. Start PowerPoint. Double-click the Help button on the Standard toolbar to display the Help Topics: Microsoft PowerPoint dialog box.
2. Click the Contents tab. Double-click the Working With Presentations book icon. Double-click What PowerPoint creates. Click the Overhead transparencies link and read the help information. Click the remaining four links and read their help information. Click the Help Topics button in the lower right corner of the Microsoft PowerPoint for Windows 95 dialog box to return to the Help Topics: Microsoft PowerPoint dialog box.
3. Click the Find tab. Type print in box 1. Click printed in box 2. Double-click Printing a presentation in box 3. When the Microsoft PowerPoint window displays, read the information, right-click the window, and click Print Topic. When the Print dialog box displays, click the OK button. Click the Close button to return to PowerPoint. Submit the printout to your instructor.

2 Expanding on the Basics

Instructions: Use PowerPoint online help to better understand the topics listed below. Begin each of the following by double-clicking the Help button on the Standard toolbar. If you cannot print the help information, answer the question on a separate piece of paper.

1. Using the Changing the Appearance of Your Presentation book icon on the Contents sheet in the Help Topics: Microsoft PowerPoint dialog box, answer the following questions. (a) How do you display the Slide Master? (b) What is the function of the Slide Master and the Title Master? and (c) How do you display an object on all slides in a presentation?
2. Using the key term, line spacing, and the Index sheet in the Help Topics: Microsoft PowerPoint dialog box, display and print the answers for the following questions. (a) How do you change the After Paragraph line spacing? (b) How do you change the amount of space within a paragraph? and (c) How do you change the alignment of all text in a text placeholder?
3. Use the Find sheet in the Help Topics: Microsoft PowerPoint dialog box to display and then print information about the function keys. Then answer the following questions: (a) Which key, or combination of keys, do you press to create a new slide? (b) Which key, or combination of keys, do you press to create a new slide without a New Slide dialog box? (c) Which key, or combination of keys, do you press to move up one paragraph? (d) Which key, or combination of keys, do you press to open a new presentation? and (e) Which key, or combination of keys, do you press to save a presentation with a different name?
4. Use the Answer Wizard sheet on the Help Topics: Microsoft PowerPoint dialog box to display and then print the information about masters. (a) How do you create a slide that is different from the Slide Master? (b) What happens to a slide when its master changes? and (c) What is master text and how do you apply it to a slide?

Apply Your Knowledge

1 Formatting a Slide

Instructions: Read the CAUTION box. Start PowerPoint. Open the presentation, Insurance Plan, from the PowerPoint folder on the Student Floppy Disk that accompanies this book. This slide lists the features of a new student insurance plan. Perform the following tasks to change the slide so it looks like the one in Figure 1-83.

1. Press and hold down the SHIFT key, and then click the Slide View button to display the Slide Master. Click the paragraph, Click to edit Master text styles. Click Format on the menu bar and then click Line Spacing. Increase the Before Paragraph line spacing to 0.75 lines. Click the OK button. Then click the Slide View button to return to Slide view.

2. Select the title text. Click the Bold button on the Formatting toolbar.

3. Select the No deductible paragraph. Click the Underline button on the Formatting toolbar.

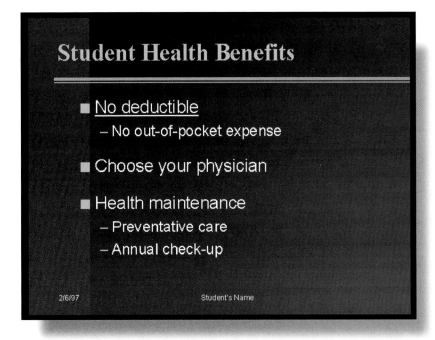

FIGURE 1-83

4. Click the paragraph, No out-of-pocket expense, and then click the Demote (Indent more) button on the Formatting toolbar. Then, demote the paragraphs, Preventative care and Annual check-up.

5. Click File on the menu bar and then click Save As. Type Student Insurance in the File name box. If drive A is not already displaying in the Save in box, click the Save in down arrow and click drive A. Then, click the Save button.

6. Click the B&W View button on the Standard toolbar to display the presentation in black and white.

7. Click the Print button on the Standard toolbar.

8. Close PowerPoint.

9. Submit the printout to your instructor.

In the Lab

1 Designing and Creating a Presentation

Problem: You are the Assistant Director for the Career Development and Placement Center at San Baarbo University. An emergency arises and you have been asked to substitute for an instructor this afternoon. The instructor suggests you discuss strategies for interviewing. To prepare for the class, you quickly create the presentation shown in Figure 1-84.

Instructions: Perform the following tasks.

1. Create a new presentation using the Bedrock Design Template.
2. Using the typewritten notes illustrated in Figure 1-85, create the title slide shown in Figure 1-84 using your name in place of Dana Fox. Decrease the font size of the paragraphs, Presented by:, Assistant Director, and Career Development Center, to 24. Increase the font size of your name to 36.
3. Using the typewritten notes in Figure 1-85, create the three multi-level bulleted list slides shown in Figure 1-84.

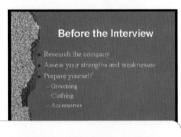

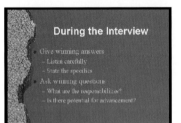

FIGURE 1-84

1)   The Successful First Interview
                Presented by: Dana Fox
                Assistant Director
                Career Development Center

2)   **Before the Interview**
        ·   Research the company
        ·   Assess your strengths and weaknesses
        ·   Prepare yourself
                *   Grooming
                *   Clothing
                *   Accessories

3)   **During the Interview**
        ·   Give winning answers
                *   Listen carefully
                *   State the specifics
        ·   Ask winning questions
                *   What are the responsibilities?
                *   Is there potential for advancement?

4)   **After the Interview**
        ·   Document interview details
        ·   Send thank you letter
        ·   Make follow-up telephone call

FIGURE 1-85

In the Lab

4. Run Style Checker to check spelling, visual clarity, and case and end punctuation. Correct your errors.
5. Save the presentation on your data floppy disk using the filename First Interview.
6. Display the presentation in black and white.
7. Print the black and white presentation.
8. Close PowerPoint.

2 Using Masters to Modify a Design Template

Problem: You are the Health & Safety Director for your company. This week's health and safety topic is Repetitive Strain Injuries. You select a Design Template but want to modify it. *Hint:* Use Help to solve this problem.

Instructions: Perform the following tasks.

1. Create a new presentation using the Blue Weave Design Template.
2. Using the notes in Figure 1-86, create the title slide shown in Figure 1-87 on the next page using your name in place of John Albrey. Decrease the font size of the paragraphs, Presented by:, and Health & Safety Director, to 24. Increase the font size of your name to 36.
3. Using the notes in Figure 1-86, create the multi-level bulleted list slides shown in Figure 1-87.
4. Display the Slide Master. Click the paragraph, Click to edit Master title style, and then click the Text Shadow button on the Formatting toolbar. Click the paragraph, Click to edit Master text styles. On the Format menu, click Line Spacing, and then increase the Before Paragraph line spacing to 0.75 lines. Drag the mouse pointer to select the paragraphs, Second level and Third level. On the Format menu, click Line Spacing, and then increase the After Paragraph spacing to 0.2 lines.

```
1)        Repetitive Strain Injuries
                   Presented by:
               John Albrey
               Health & Safety Director

2)        What Is Repetitive Strain Injury (RSI)?
          .        Injury to the hands and/or wrists
                   *        Tendons or muscles are strained or torn
                   *        Blood circulation is impaired
                   *        Tissues deprived of nutrients
                   *        Toxins allowed to build

3)        Who Gets RSI?
          .        People with jobs that require repetitive hand or wrist motion
          .        Examples:
                   *        Computer users
                   *        Typists
                   *        Assembly-line workers
                   *        Meat cutters

4)        How Do You Prevent RSI?
          .        Before Work
                   *        Perform wrist and hand warm-up exercises
          .        During Work
                   *        Relax and keep hands warm
                   *        Maintain good posture
                   *        Keep wrists and forearms parallel to floor
```

FIGURE 1-86

(continued)

In the Lab

Using Masters to Modify a Design Template *(continued)*

5. Drag the elevator to display the Title Master. Click the paragraph, Click to edit Master title style, and then click the Text Shadow button on the Formatting toolbar. On the View menu, click Header and Footer. Then add the current date, slide number, and your name to the footer. Display the footer on all slides. Return to Slide view.

FIGURE 1-87

6. Run Style Checker to check spelling, visual larity, and case and end punctuation. Correct your errors.
7. Drag the elevator to display Slide 1. Click the Slide Show button to start Slide Show view. Then click to display each slide.
8. Save the presentation on your data floppy disk using the filename, Repetitive Strain Injuries.
9. Display and print the presentation in black and white.
10. Close PowerPoint.

3 Creating a Training Presentation

Problem: You are a financial planner conducting a personal finance seminar. Over the years, you have accumulated many proven methods for saving money and spending less.

Instructions: Using the list in Figure 1-88, design and create a presentation. The presentation is to include a title slide and five bulleted list slides. Modify the list to conform to Style Checker defaults. Perform the following tasks:

1. Create a new presentation using the Blue Green Design Template.
2. Create a title slide titled Money. Include Are You Saving or Slaving? as the subtitle.
3. Using Figure 1-88, create five multi-level bulleted list slides. Modify the list illustrated in Figure 1-88 to conform to Style Checker defaults (see Table 1-5 on PP 1.44).

In the Lab

4. Adjust Before Paragraph and After Paragraph line spacing to utilize the available white space.
5. Save the presentation to your data floppy disk with the filename Money.
6. View the presentation in Slide Show view to look for errors. Correct any errors.
7. Print the presentation in black and white.
8. Close PowerPoint.

Money
Are You Saving or Slaving?

I. **Saving Savvy**
   A.   Save consistently
        1.   Deposit a little money every week
           a)   Saving $10 a week easier than $40 a month
        2.   Use payroll deductions
           a)   Savings bonds
           b)   401K plan
           c)   Thrift plan
        3.   Make savings part of your budget
           a)   Deposit cash saved from discounts
   B.   Open specialty savings accounts
        1.   Vacation club
        2.   College fund
        3.   Christmas club

II. **Reduce Finance Charges**
   A.   Pay cash
        1.   Don't create additional debt
        2.   Save until you can pay cash for an item
   B.   Eliminate high interest debt
        1.   Make larger payments
           a)   Pay more then minimum amount due
           b)   Make more frequent payments
               (1)   Make bimonthly payments
               (2)   Make weekly payments
        2.   Consolidate bills
           a)   Eliminate several bills into one
           b)   Refinance at lower interest rate

III. **Food Savings**
   A.   Brown-bag your lunch
        1.   Plan meals for entire week
        2.   Use restaurant "doggie-bag" leftovers for next day's lunch
   B.   Grocery shop from a list
        1.   Resist impulse buying
           a)   Don't shop when hungry
        2.   Read cost-per-unit labels
        3.   Use coupons for what you normally buy
           a)   Don't buy an item because you have a coupon
        4.   Buy in bulk
           a)   Only if you'll use before it spoils

IV. **Car Savings**
   A.   Insurance
        1.   Insure all cars with same company
           a)   Look for 15 to 20 percent discount
        2.   Reduce coverage on old cars
           a)   Consider eliminating collision coverage
   B.   Maintenance
        1.   Read warranty carefully
           a)   Dealer might be required to fix
        2.   Buy supplies at discount stores
        3.   Do minor repairs yourself
   C.   Driving
        1.   Get ready before you start engine
           a)   Adjust mirrors and seat
           b)   Fasten seatbelt
        2.   Gradually increase and decrease speed

V. **Bill Paying Strategy**
   A.   Organize bills
   B.   Write check when bill arrives
        1.   Mail just before due date
   C.   Don't skip payments
        1.   Send small amounts to every creditor
        2.   Call creditor if you must pay late

FIGURE 1-88

Cases and Places

200 MHz

The difficulty of these case studies varies:

▶ Case studies preceded by a single half moon are the least difficult. You are asked to create the required presentation based on information that has already been placed in an organized form.

▶▶ Case studies preceded by two half moons are more difficult. You must organize the information given before using it to create the required presentation.

▶▶▶ Case studies preceded by three half moons are the most difficult. You must decide on a specific topic, and then obtain and organize the necessary information before using it to create the required presentation.

1 ▶ Pauline Gauguin, an art instructor from the Synthétiste School, is giving a presentation at the next parent-teachers meeting. She has written out a recipe for finger paint (Figure 1-89).

With this recipe, Ms. Gauguin has asked you to prepare four slides that can be used on an overhead projector. Use the concepts and techniques introduced in this project to create the presentation.

Homemade Finger Paint

Ingredients
✔ *1/3 cup cornstarch*
✔ *3 cups sugar*
✔ *2 cups cold water*
✔ *food color*

Preparation
✔ *Mix cornstarch, sugar, and water*
  Use 1-quart saucepan
✔ *Cover and stir over medium heat*
  About 5 minutes or until thickened
✔ *Remove from heat*

Adding Color
✔ *Divide mixture into separate cups*
✔ *Tint each cup with a different food color*
  Stir several times until cool
✔ *Store in airtight container*
  Paint works best if used the same day

FIGURE 1-89

Cases and Places

2 ▶ Bill Henry, managing director for the Skoon County Fair, has prepared some notes for a presentation that will be given to the local chamber of commerce (Figure 1-90).

With these notes, the fair director has asked you to prepare four slides that can be used on an overhead projector. Use the concepts and techniques introduced in this project to create the presentation.

25th Annual Skoon County Fair

P.B. Pillbottom's Midway
- *Over 50 rides and attractions*
  World's largest carousel ·
- *Games of skill and chance ·*
- *The Kiddie Corral*
  Activities for children under 8
Popular Exhibits ·
- *Arts and crafts*
  Prizes in 32 separate categories ·
- *Domesticated animals*
  Prizes in 26 classes ·
- *Commercial demonstrations*
Family Entertainment ·
- *The Neighborhood Bigtop*
  Bring a camera to film the kids ·
- *Western Rodeo Jamboree ·*
- *Music and shows*
  The Bronco Brothers
  "Thank God I'm a Country Boy"

FIGURE 1-90

3 ▶▶ As part of a symposium on the history of American education, you are giving a presentation on the Curriculum of General Schools, as proposed in a letter by Thomas Jefferson to Peter Carr. Jefferson divides the general school curriculum into three departments—language, mathematics, and philosophy. The language department is composed of languages and history (both may be attained by the same course of reading), grammar, belles lettres (poetry, composition, and criticism), and rhetoric and oratory. The department of mathematics includes: mathematics pure, physico-mathematics (physical subjects aided by mathematical calculation), natural history (mineralogy, botany, zoology, and anatomy), and the theory of medicine. The philosophical department encompasses ideology, ethics, law of nature and nations, and government (political economy). In addition to a title slide, you plan to develop three other slides that can be used with an overhead projector. Use the concepts and techniques introduced in this project to create the presentation.

Cases and Places

4 ▶▶ You are a consultant in the field of ergonomics (an applied science devoted to making the equipment people use and the surrounding work area safer and more efficient). You have been hired by a large company to give a presentation on Computer User Health Guidelines, and you have been asked to cover three topics—a well-designed work area, equipment in the workplace, and ways to reduce physical and mental fatigue. A well-designed work area contains a desk approximately 30 inches high; a chair with adjustable backrest, seat, and height and 5 legs for stability; and adequate lighting using nonglare bulbs. Equipment in the workplace should consist of a keyboard at a height apropos to the height of the operator; a monitor at a viewing distance between 18 and 28 inches (a viewing angle of 20° to center of screen); a monitor designed to minimize electromagnetic radiation (EMR); and a document holder placed at the same height and distance as screen. Ways to reduce physical and mental fatigue are to alternate work activities (change the order of work to provide variety); minimize surrounding noise; take frequent breaks (look away from the screen every 15 minutes, get out of the chair at least once each hour, and take a 15 minute break every two hours); and incorporate stretching exercises into breaks. In addition to a title slide, you plan to develop three other slides that can be used with an overhead projector. Use the concepts and techniques introduced in this project to create the presentation.

5 ▶▶▶ Appreciation of local landmarks—historical sites, museums, or natural wonders—often can be increased by a preliminary presentation. Go to an area landmark and gather information on its significance, history, popularity, etc. Using this information, together with the concepts and techniques introduced in this project, prepare a presentation to familiarize visitors with the landmark. Create a title slide and at least three other slides that can be used with an overhead projector to enhance the presentation.

6 ▶▶▶ Some instructors use the first class meeting to provide a broad orientation for their students. At this time, students may learn about course requirements, grading policies, academic deadlines, necessary supplies, or the instructor's office hours. Choose a class you are currently taking and outline the information you feel should be offered to students on the first day of class. Using this information, together with the concepts and techniques introduced in this project, prepare a presentation to orient students on opening day. Create a title slide and at least three other slides that can be used with an overhead projector to enhance the presentation.

7 ▶▶▶ Schools often purchase computer equipment on the basis of a sales representative's presentation. Visit a computer vendor and select the system you feel is most appropriate for an elementary school. Determine the features that would make this system attractive to a grade school, such as ease of use, suitability of software, processing power, and available peripheral devices. Using this information, together with the concepts and techniques introduced in this project, prepare a presentation to sell the system to an elementary school's staff. Create a title slide and at least three other slides that can be used with an overhead projector to enhance the presentation.

Microsoft PowerPoint 7

Using Outline View and Clip Art to Create an Electronic Slide Show

Objectives:

You will have mastered the material in this project when you can:

▶ Create a presentation in Outline view
▶ Describe the PowerPoint window in Outline view
▶ Insert a blank line in a bulleted list
▶ Change the slide layout
▶ Move text between objects
▶ Insert clip art from the ClipArt Gallery
▶ Change the clip art size
▶ Add a header and a footer to outline pages
▶ Add slide transition effects
▶ Add text build effects
▶ Print a presentation outline
▶ Change printing options
▶ Change the slide order
▶ Copy a slide

Making a Point

The Mad Hatter was right, of course. If Alice meant to say one thing and said something else, no matter how much she meant it, she failed to make her point . . . or at least, made the wrong point.

Every day, in countless diverse situations, speakers are faced with the daunting task of making a point with words. Fortunately, over the years of human history, people have learned an important principle: words go down better with a spoonful of graphics!

Speakers today have an advantage over their predecessors who seldom had the benefit of sparkling visuals to help them make a point. With the double-barreled impact of words teamed up with pictures, a point is made — then made again. Another subtle benefit also is

"Then you should say what you mean," the March Hare went on.

"I do," Alice hastily replied, "at least — at least I mean what I say — that's the same thing, you know."

"Not the same thing a bit!" said the Mad Hatter.

Alice in Wonderland by Lewis Carroll

present: good graphics can help a speaker stay on track and on target. Practically everyone, from political candidate to college student to general to salesperson, has the means to create dynamic, attractive slide presentations to reinforce verbal remarks.

Armed with presentation graphics software, a user can generate a complete slide presentation often in less time than it takes to write a speech. Visuals may become the thematic focal points of a paper or oral presentation, around which one or more ideas can be built with written text or speech. By clearly establishing the expectations of the reader or listener, a picture can be the "point guard" for the ideas that follow.

General Norman Schwarzkopf, Marcia Clark, Ross Perot, and every U.S. president from Lyndon Johnson to Bill Clinton are just a few of the famous people who have used computer-generated graphics to emphasize or clarify their remarks.

College students not only are able to make a point, but are able to make *grade* points, as well, using computer-generated graphics in virtually any kind of course, whether for inclusion in a paper or an oral presentation. Every day, sales people deliver countless stand-up presentations using graphic slides to underscore each of their points, known as features and bene-fits. Aircraft engineers use graphics to point out the charac-teristics of supersonic aircraft.

In a competitive world, Microsoft PowerPoint and every other available tool should be used to make an argument more persuasive. Then, upon yielding the floor, to hear someone say, "A point well-taken... ," that is the ultimate reward.

Microsoft
PowerPoint 7
Windows 95

Using Outline View and Clip Art to Create an Electronic Slide Show

*C*ase *P*erspective

Web Island Resort is promoting Web Island to college students as *the* place for spring break vacations. While developing a presentation to promote two new spring break vacation packages to Web Island, your boss, Mr. Hayes, receives a telephone call. During the call, Western University invites Web Island Resort to make a presentation at their Spring Break Vacation Fair. For some unspecified reason, another resort is canceling, thereby giving Web Island Resort an opportunity to present. The Vacation Fair is tomorrow. In order for Mr. Hayes to finalize his travel arrangements, he asks you to put together a short six slide presentation. The purpose of the presentation is to entice students to buy one of the spring break vacation packages.

Web Island Resort's Marketing Department supplies you with an outline to use to create the presentation. The outline contains promotional information about the new spring break vacation packages.

To persuade students to buy a Web Island Resort spring break vacation package, you choose a design template with a tropical theme. You also include pictures to intensify the text.

*C*reating a Presentation from an Outline

At some time during either your academic or business life, you probably will make a presentation. Most academic presentations are informative—providing detailed information about some topic. Business presentations, however, are usually sales presentations, such as selling a proposal or a product to a client, convincing management to approve a new project, or persuading the board of directors to accept the fiscal budget. As an alternative to creating your presentation in Slide view, as you did in Project 1, PowerPoint provides an outlining feature to help you organize your thoughts. When the outline is complete, it becomes the foundation for your presentation.

You create a presentation outline in Outline view. When you create an outline, you type all of your text at one time, as if you were typing an outline on a sheet of paper. This is different than Slide view where you type text as you create each individual slide.

The first step in creating a presentation in Outline view is to type a title for the outline. The outline title is the subject of the presentation and later becomes the presentation title slide. Then you type the remainder of the outline, indenting appropriately to establish a structure or hierarchy. Once the outline is complete, you make your presentation more persuasive by adding graphics. This project uses outlining to create the presentation and clip art graphics to visually support the text.

Project Two – Spring Break Specials

Project 2 uses PowerPoint to create the six slide Web Island Resort Spring Break Specials presentation shown in Figure 2-1. You create the presentation from the outline in Figure 2-2 on the next page.

FIGURES 2-1a

FIGURES 2-1b

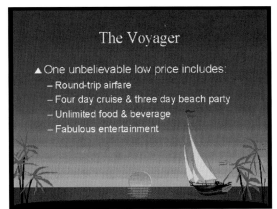

FIGURES 2-1c

FIGURES 2-1f

FIGURES 2-1d

FIGURES 2-1e

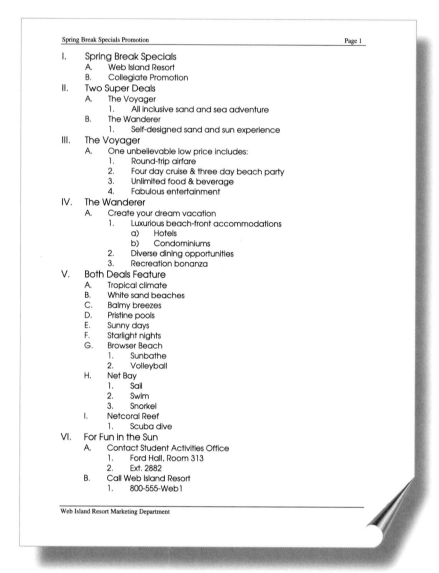

Spring Break Specials Promotion   Page 1

I.   Spring Break Specials
     A.   Web Island Resort
     B.   Collegiate Promotion
II. Two Super Deals
     A.   The Voyager
          1.   All inclusive sand and sea adventure
     B.   The Wanderer
          1.   Self-designed sand and sun experience
III. The Voyager
     A.   One unbelievable low price includes:
          1.   Round-trip airfare
          2.   Four day cruise & three day beach party
          3.   Unlimited food & beverage
          4.   Fabulous entertainment
IV. The Wanderer
     A.   Create your dream vacation
          1.   Luxurious beach-front accommodations
               a)   Hotels
               b)   Condominiums
          2.   Diverse dining opportunities
          3.   Recreation bonanza
V.   Both Deals Feature
     A.   Tropical climate
     B.   White sand beaches
     C.   Balmy breezes
     D.   Pristine pools
     E.   Sunny days
     F.   Starlight nights
     G.   Browser Beach
          1.   Sunbathe
          2.   Volleyball
     H.   Net Bay
          1.   Sail
          2.   Swim
          3.   Snorkel
     I.   Netcoral Reef
          1.   Scuba dive
VI. For Fun in the Sun
     A.   Contact Student Activities Office
          1.   Ford Hall, Room 313
          2.   Ext. 2882
     B.   Call Web Island Resort
          1.   800-555-Web1

Web Island Resort Marketing Department

FIGURE 2-2

Presentation Preparation Steps

The preparation steps summarize how the slide presentation shown in Figure 2-1 on page PP 2.5 will be developed in Project 2. The following tasks will be completed in this project.

1. Start a new document and apply a Design Template.
2. Create a presentation in Outline view.
3. Save the presentation.
4. Insert a blank line on Slide 2.
5. Change the Slide 5 layout to 2 Column Text and move text from the left column to the right column.
6. Change the Slide 6 layout to Clip Art and Text and insert a clip art picture into a clip art placeholder.
7. Insert clip art in Slide 3. Move and reduce the size of the clip art picture.
8. Add header and footer text to the outline pages.
9. Add slide transition effects and text build effects.

10. Save the presentation.
11. Print the presentation outline and slides.
12. Edit the presentation in Outline view and in Slide Sorter view.
13. Close PowerPoint.

The following pages contain a detailed explanation of these tasks.

Starting a New Presentation

Project 1 introduced you to starting a presentation document and applying a Design Template. The following steps summarize how to start a new presentation, apply a Design Template, and choose an AutoLayout. For a more detailed explanation, see pages PP 1.9 through PP 1.12. Perform the following steps to start a new presentation.

TO START A NEW PRESENTATION

Step 1: Click the Start button on the taskbar.
Step 2: Click New Office Document.
Step 3: Click the Presentation Designs tab. When the Presentation Designs sheet displays, scroll down the list of Design Templates until Tropical displays.
Step 4: Double-click Tropical.
Step 5: When the New Slide dialog box displays, click the OK button.

PowerPoint displays the Title Slide AutoLayout and the Tropical Design Template on Slide 1 in Slide View (Figure 2-3).

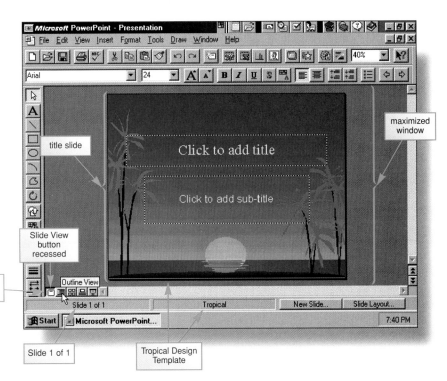

FIGURE 2-3

Using Outline View

Outline view provides a quick, easy way to create a presentation. Outlining allows you to organize your thoughts in a structured format. An outline uses indentation to establish a hierarchy, which denotes levels of importance to the main topic. An **outline** is a summary of thoughts, presented as headings and subheadings, often used as a preliminary draft when you create a presentation.

More *About* **Design Templates**

You can build a presentation with the default Design Template and later select a different one. When you change Design Templates, PowerPoint automatically updates color scheme, font attributes, and location of slide objects on every slide in the presentation.

In Outline view, title text displays at the left side of the window along with a slide icon and a slide number. Body text is indented under the title text. Graphic objects, such as pictures, graphs, or tables, do not display in Outline view. When a slide contains a graphic object, the slide icon next to the slide title displays with a small graphic on it. The slide icon is blank when a slide does not contain graphics. The attributes for text in Outline view are the same as in Slide view except for color and paragraph style.

PowerPoint limits the number of outline levels to six. The first outline level is the slide title. The remaining five outline levels are the same as the five indent levels in Slide view. Recall from Project 1 that PowerPoint allows for five indent levels and that each indent level has an associated bullet.

The outline begins with a title on **outline level one**. The title is the main topic of the slide. Text supporting the main topic begins on **outline level two** and indents under outline level one. **Outline level three** indents under outline level two and contains text to support outline level two. **Outline level four**, **outline level five**, and **outline level six** indent under outline level three, outline level four, and outline level five, respectively. Use outline levels four, five, and six as required. They are generally used for scientific and engineering presentations requiring vast amounts of detail. Business and sales presentations usually focus on summary information and use outline level one, outline level two, and outline level three.

PowerPoint initially displays in Slide view when you start a new presentation. Change from Slide view to Outline view by clicking the Outline View button on the View Button bar. Perform the following steps to change the view from Slide view to Outline view.

Steps **To Change the View to Outline View**

1 **Point to the Outline View button located on the View Button bar at the lower-left of the PowerPoint window (Figure 2-4).**

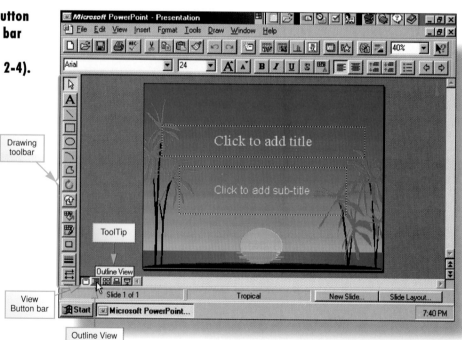

FIGURE 2-4

2 **Click the Outline View button.**

PowerPoint displays the Outline View window (Figure 2-5).

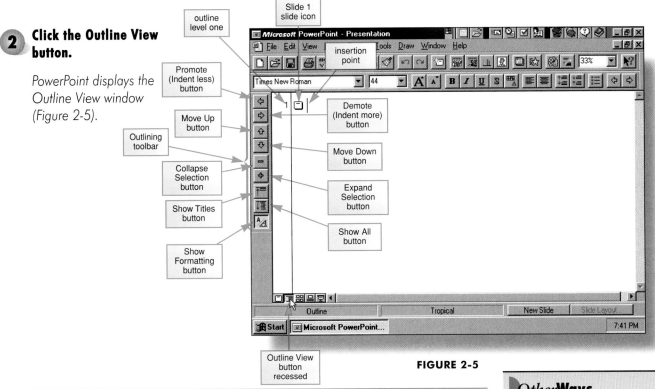

FIGURE 2-5

You can create and edit your presentation in Outline view. Outline view also makes it easy to sequence slides and to relocate title text and body text from one slide to another. In addition to typing text to create a new presentation in Outline view, PowerPoint can produce slides from an outline created in Microsoft Word or another word processor, if you save the outline as an RTF file or as a plain text file. The file extension **RTF** stands for **R**ich **T**ext **F**ormat.

The PowerPoint Window in Outline View

The PowerPoint window in Outline view differs from the window in Slide view because the Outlining toolbar displays and the Drawing toolbar does not display (see Figures 2-4 and 2-5). Table 2-1 on the next page describes the buttons on the Outlining toolbar.

Other Ways

1. On menu bar click View, click Outline
2. Press ALT+V, press O

More *About* **Outline Levels**

A topic needing more than six outline levels has too much detail and may overwhelm the audience. Decompose large topics into two or more subtopics. Then, create a new slide for each group of subtopics.

Table 2-1

BUTTON	BUTTON NAME	DESCRIPTION
	Promote button	The Promote (Indent less) button moves the selected paragraph up one level in the outline hierarchy each time you click the button. Promoting a paragraph moves it to the left until you reach outline level one.
	Demote button	The Demote (Indent more) button moves the selected paragraph down, or to the right, one level in the outline hierarchy each time you click the button. You can only demote to the sixth outline level.
	Move Up button	The Move Up button moves selected text up one paragraph at a time while maintaining its hierarchical outline level and text style. The selected text exchanges position with the paragraph located above it.
	Move Down button	The Move Down button moves selected text down one paragraph at time while maintaining its hierarchical outline level and text style. The selected text exchanges position with the paragraph located below it.
	Collapse Selection button	The Collapse Selection button hides all outline levels except the slide title of the selected slide. This button is useful when you want to collapse one slide in your outline.
	Expand Selection button	The Expand Selection button displays all outline levels for the selected slide. This button is useful when you want to expand one slide in your outline.
	Show Titles button	The Show Titles button collapses all outline levels to show only the slide titles. This button is useful when you are looking at the organization of your presentation and do not care to see all the details.
	Show All button	The Show All button expands all outline levels to display the title and text for all slides.
	Show Formatting button	The Show Formatting button is a toggle that displays or hides the text attributes in Outline view. This is useful when you want to work with plain text as opposed to working with bolded, italicized, or underlined text. When printing your outline, plain text often speeds up the printing process.

Creating a Presentation in Outline View

Outline view enables you to view title and body text, add and delete slides, **drag and drop** slide text, drag and drop slides to change slide order, promote and demote text, save a presentation, print an outline, print slides, copy and paste slides or text to and from other presentations, apply a Design Template, and import an outline.

Developing a presentation in Outline view is quick because you type the text for all slides on one screen. Once you type the outline, the presentation is fundamentally complete. If you choose, you can then go to Slide view to enhance your presentation with graphics.

Creating a Title Slide in Outline View

Recall from Project 1 that the title slide introduces the presentation to the audience. Additionally, Project 2 uses the title slide to capture the attention of the audience by using a Design Template with a tropical theme. The Tropical Design Template enhances the presentation title with tropical plants and a setting sun. Remember, Web Island Resort is trying to sell vacation packages. They want students to focus on a warm, tropical climate. Perform the following steps to create a title slide in Outline view.

Steps To Create a Title Slide in Outline View

1 **Type** Spring Break Specials **and press the ENTER key.**

Spring Break Specials displays as the title for Slide 1 and is called outline level one. A slide icon displays to the left of each slide title. The font for outline level one is Times New Roman and the font size is 44 points. In Outline view, the Zoom Control default setting is 33% of the actual slide size. Pressing the ENTER key moves the insertion point to the next line and maintains the same outline level. The insertion point, therefore, is in position for typing the title for Slide 2 (Figure 2-6).

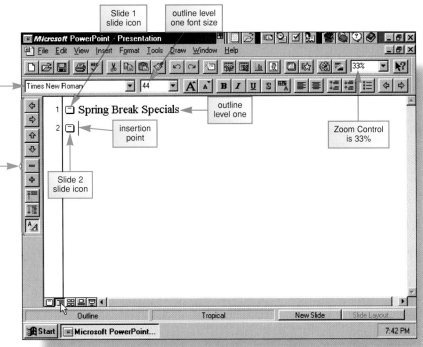

FIGURE 2-6

2 **Point to the Demote (Indent more) button on the Outlining toolbar.**

The Demote (Indent more) ToolTip displays (Figure 2-7).

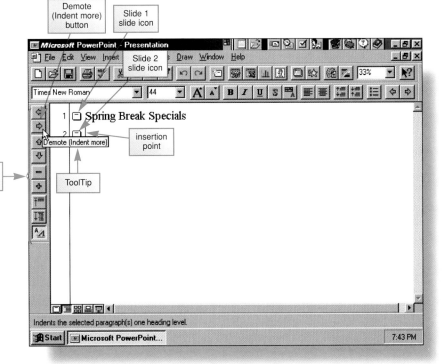

FIGURE 2-7

3 **Click the Demote (Indent more) button. Type** Web Island Resort **and press the ENTER key. Type** Collegiate Promotion **and press the ENTER key.**

The Slide 2 slide icon does not display (Figure 2-8). The lines, Web Island Resort and Collegiate Promotion, are subtitles on the title slide (Slide 1) and demote to outline level two. Outline level two is indented to the right under outline level one. The outline level two font is Arial and the outline level two font size is 32 points.

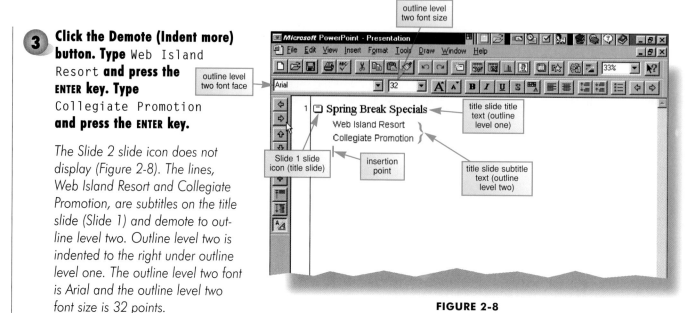

FIGURE 2-8

The title slide for the Spring Break Specials presentation is complete. The next section explains how to add a slide in Outline view.

Adding a Slide in Outline View

Recall from Project 1 that when you add a new slide, PowerPoint defaults to the Bulleted List slide layout. This is true in Outline view as well. One way to add a new slide in Outline view is to promote a paragraph to outline level one. You do this by clicking the Promote (Indent less) button until the insertion point is at outline level one. A slide icon displays when you reach outline level one. Perform the following steps to add a slide in Outline view.

Steps **To Add a Slide in Outline View**

1 **Point to the Promote (Indent less) button on the Outlining toolbar.**

The insertion point is still positioned at outline level two (Figure 2-9).

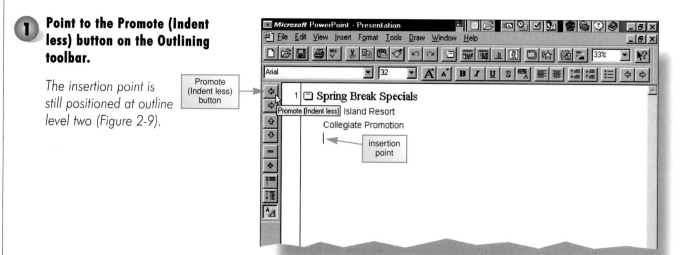

FIGURE 2-9

2 **Click the Promote (Indent less) button.**

The Slide 2 slide icon displays indicating a new slide is added to the presentation (Figure 2-10). The insertion point is in position to type the title for Slide 2 at outline level one.

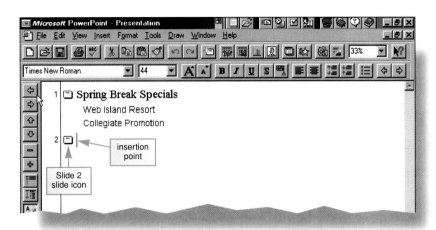

FIGURE 2-10

After you add a slide, you are ready to type the slide text. The next section explains how to create a multi-level bulleted list slide in Outline view.

Creating Multi-level Bulleted List Slides in Outline View

To create a multi-level bulleted list slide, you demote or promote the insertion point to the appropriate outline level and then type the paragraph text. Recall from Project 1, when you demote a paragraph, PowerPoint adds a bullet to the left of each outline level. Each outline level has a different bullet font. Also recall that the Design Template determines font attributes, including the bullet font.

Slide 2 is the first informational slide for Project 2. Slide 2 introduces the main topic — two new spring break vacation packages offered by Web Island Resort. Each vacation package displays as outline level two, and each supportive paragraph displays as outline level three. The following steps explain how to create a multi-level bulleted list slide in Outline view.

Steps To Create a Multi-level Slide in Outline View

1 **Type** Two Super Deals **and press the ENTER key. Then click the Demote (Indent more) button to demote to outline level two.**

The title for Slide 2, Two Super Deals, displays and the insertion point is in position to type the first bulleted paragraph (Figure 2-11). A triangle shaped bullet displays to the left of the insertion point.

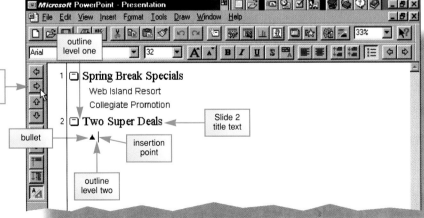

FIGURE 2-11

2 **Type** The Voyager **and press the ENTER key. Then click the Demote (Indent more) button to demote to outline level three.**

Slide 2 displays three outline levels: the title, Two Super Deals, on outline level one, the bulleted paragraph, The Voyager, on outline level two, and the insertion point on outline level three (Figure 2-12). The bullet for outline level two is a triangle. The bullet for outline level three is a dash.

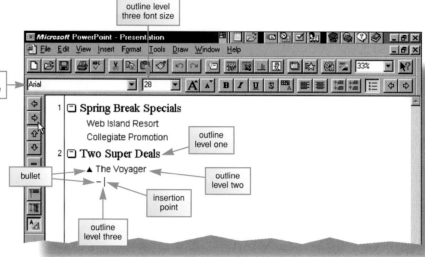

FIGURE 2-12

3 **Type** All inclusive sand and sea adventure **and press the ENTER key. Then click the Promote (Indent less) button.**

Pressing the ENTER key begins a new paragraph at the same outline level as the previous paragraph. Clicking the Promote (Indent less) button moves the insertion point left and elevates the paragraph from outline level three to outline level two (Figure 2-13).

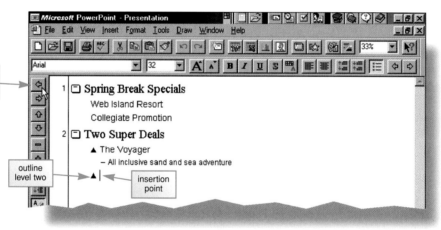

FIGURE 2-13

4 **Type** The Wanderer **and press the ENTER key. Click the Demote (Indent more) button. Type** Self-designed sand and sun experience **and press the ENTER key (Figure 2-14).**

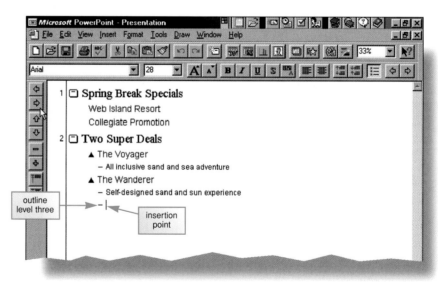

FIGURE 2-14

OtherWays

1. Press TAB to Demote
2. Press ALT+SHIFT+RIGHT ARROW to Demote

OtherWays

1. Press SHIFT+TAB to Promote
2. Press ALT+SHIFT+LEFT ARROW to Promote

Creating a Subordinate Slide

When developing your presentation, begin with a main topic and follow with subsequent slides to support the main topic. Placing all your information on one slide may overwhelm your audience. Decompose your presentation, therefore, into several slides with three to six bullets per slide or per object. The following steps explain how to create a subordinate slide that further explains the spring break package, The Voyager, introduced on Slide 2. This new slide, Slide 3, provides additional information that supports the first outline level two on Slide 2. Later in this project, you will create another subordinate slide to support the second outline level two on Slide 2, The Wanderer.

TO CREATE A SUBORDINATE SLIDE

Step 1: Click the Promote (Indent less) button two times so that Slide 3 is added to the end of the presentation.

Step 2: Type The Voyager and press the ENTER key.

Step 3: Click the Demote (Indent more) button to demote to outline level two.

Step 4: Type One unbelievable low price includes: and press the ENTER key.

Step 5: Click the Demote (Indent more) button to demote to outline level three.

Step 6: Type Round-trip airfare and press the ENTER key.

Step 7: Type Four day cruise & three day beach party and press the ENTER key.

Step 8: Type Unlimited food & beverage and press the ENTER key.

Step 9: Type Fabulous entertainment and press the ENTER key.

The screen displays as shown in Figure 2-15.

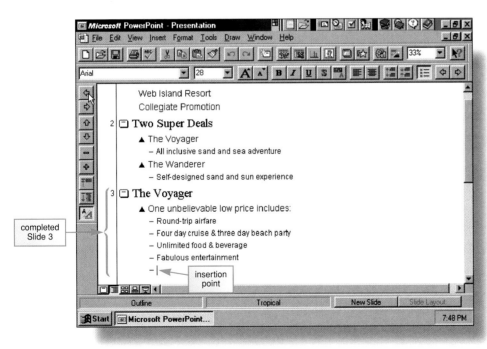

FIGURE 2-15

Creating a Second Subordinate Slide

The next step is to create the slide that supports The Wanderer, which is the second outline level two on Slide 2. Perform the following steps to create this subordinate slide.

TO CREATE A SECOND SUBORDINATE SLIDE

Step 1: Click the Promote (Indent less) button two times so that Slide 4 is added to the end of the presentation. Type The Wanderer and press the ENTER key.

Step 2: Click the Demote (Indent more) button to demote to outline level two. Type Create your dream vacation and press the ENTER key.

Step 3: Click the Demote (Indent more) button to demote to outline level three. Type Luxurious beach-front accommodations and press the ENTER key.

Step 4: Click the Demote (Indent more) button to demote to outline level four. Type Hotels and press the ENTER key. Type Condominiums and press the ENTER key.

Step 5: Click the Promote (Indent less) button to promote to outline level three. Type Diverse dining opportunities and press the ENTER key. Type Recreation bonanza and press the ENTER key.

The screen displays as shown in Figure 2-16.

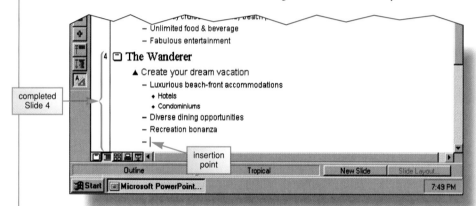

completed
Slide 4

FIGURE 2-16

Creating a Slide with Multiple Text Objects in Outline View

All of the slides you have created to this point consist of a title object and one text object. Occasionally, you need to provide the audience with a long list of items. If you use the Bulleted List slide layout, Style Checker will identify the slide as having too many bullets. Recall from Project 1 that Style Checker checks a presentation for spelling, visual clarity, and end punctuation. One of the design standards Style Checker looks for is too many bullets in an object.

In order to create a slide with more than six bulleted paragraphs and still comply with design standards, break the list into two or more objects. When you divide the text into multiple objects, each object complies with PowerPoint's default settings for visual clarity in Style Checker, as long as the number of bullets per object is less than or equal to six. Six is the default setting for the number of bullets per object.

Because you are creating the presentation in Outline view, type the text for this slide as a bulleted list. Later in this project, you convert the bulleted list slide into a multiple object slide by changing views, changing slide layout, and moving some of the text from the bulleted list to another object. Perform the steps below to create a slide with multiple text objects in Outline view.

TO CREATE A SLIDE WITH MULTIPLE TEXT OBJECTS IN OUTLINE VIEW

Step 1: Click the Promote (Indent less) button two times so that Slide 5 is added to the end of the presentation. Type Both Deals Feature as the slide title and press the ENTER key.

Step 2: Click the Demote (Indent more) button to demote to outline level two. Type Tropical climate and press the ENTER key. Type White sand beaches and press the ENTER key. Type Balmy breezes and press the ENTER key. Type Pristine pools and press the ENTER key. Type Sunny days and press the ENTER key. Type Starlight nights and press the ENTER key. Type Browser Beach and press the ENTER key.

Step 3: Click the Demote (Indent more) button to demote to outline level three. Type Sunbathe, volleyball and press the ENTER key.

Step 4: Click the Promote (Indent less) button to promote to outline level two. Type Net Bay and press the ENTER key.

Step 5: Click the Demote (Indent more) button to demote to outline level three. Type Sail, swim, snorkel and press the ENTER key

Step 6: Click the Promote (Indent less) button to promote to outline level two. Type Net Coral Reef and press the ENTER key.

Step 7: Click the Demote (Indent more) button to demote to outline level three. Type Scuba dive and press the ENTER key.

The screen displays as shown in Figure 2-17.

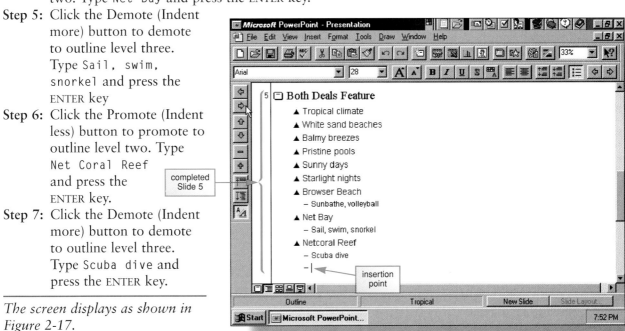

FIGURE 2-17

Creating a Closing Slide in Outline View

The last slide in your presentation is the **closing slide**. A closing slide gracefully ends a presentation. Often used during a question and answer session, the closing slide usually remains on the screen to reinforce the message delivered during the presentation. Professional speakers design the closing slide with one or more of the methods on the next page.

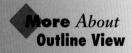

More *About*
Outline View

When working in Outline view, many people prefer to use keyboard keys instead of toolbar buttons. This way their hands never leave the keyboard and their typing is finished more quickly. For example, instead of clicking the Demote button to demote text, press the TAB key.

1. List important information. Tell the audience what to do next.
2. Provide a memorable illustration or example to make a point.
3. Appeal to emotions. Remind the audience to take action or accept responsibility.
4. Summarize the main points of the presentation.
5. Cite a quotation that directly relates to the main points of the presentation. This is most effective if the presentation started with a quotation.

The closing slide in this project combines listing important information and providing an illustration. Because Web Island Resort wants students to buy one of the tropical island vacations, they combine telling students what to do next with providing a list of telephone numbers on the Tropical Design Template. In this presentation, the design template serves as a recurrent illustration. Perform the following steps to create this closing slide.

TO CREATE A CLOSING SLIDE IN OUTLINE VIEW

Step 1: Click the Promote (Indent less) button two times so that Slide 6 is added to the end of the presentation. Type For Fun in the Sun as the slide title and press the ENTER key.

Step 2: Click the Demote (Indent more) button to demote to outline level two. Type Contact Student Activities Office and press the ENTER key.

Step 3: Click the Demote (Indent more) button to demote to outline level three. Type Ford Hall, Room 313 and press the ENTER key. Type Ext. 2882 and press the ENTER key.

Step 4: Click the Promote (Indent less) button to promote to outline level two. Type Call Web Island Resort and press the ENTER key.

Step 5: Click the Demote (Indent more) button to demote to outline level three. Type 800-555-Web1 but do not press the ENTER key.

Slide 6 displays as shown in Figure 2-18.

The outline is now complete and the presentation should be saved. The next section explains how to save the presentation.

Saving the Presentation

Recall from Project 1 that it is wise to frequently save your presentation on disk. Because you have created all the text for your presentation, you should save your presentation now. For a detailed explanation of the steps summarized on the next page, refer to pages PP 1.22 through PP 1.24 in Project 1.

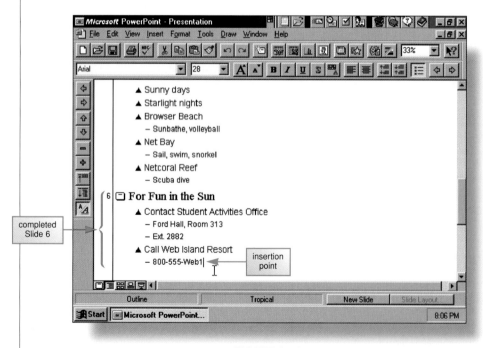

FIGURE 2-18

TO SAVE A PRESENTATION

Step 1: Insert a formatted floppy disk in drive A. Then click the Save button on the Standard toolbar.
Step 2: Type Spring Break Specials in the File Name box. Do not press the ENTER key.
Step 3: Click the Save in down arrow. Click 3½ Floppy [A:] in the Save in drop-down list.
Step 4: Click the Save button.

The presentation is saved to drive A under the name Spring Break Specials.

Reviewing a Presentation in Slide Sorter View

When you create a presentation in Outline view, only the text is visible. You cannot see how the text looks on the slide nor how the design template affects the text objects. You must, therefore, see how the text looks on the slides to evaluate necessary changes. Changing to Slide Sorter view allows you to display your presentation slides in miniature so that you can quickly review the slides for content, organization, and overall appearance.

In Project 1, you displayed slides in Slide Show view to look at individual slides. Slide Show view limits you to looking at one slide at a time. Slide Sorter view, however, allows you to look at several slides at one time, which is helpful when you review your presentation for slide order. You will learn how to change slide order in Slide Sorter view later in this project. Perform the following steps to change from Outline view to Slide Sorter view.

Steps — To Change the View to Slide Sorter View

1 Point to the Slide Sorter View button on the View Button bar at the bottom of the PowerPoint window (Figure 2-19).

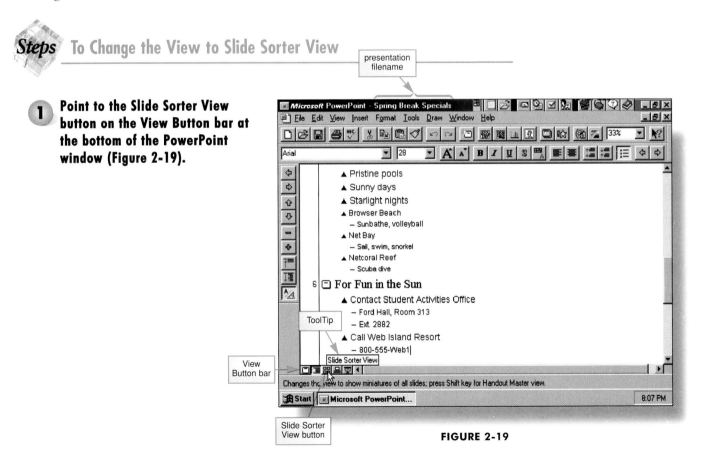

FIGURE 2-19

2 **Click the Slide Sorter View button.**

PowerPoint displays the presentation in Slide Sorter view (Figure 2-20). Slide 6 is selected because it was the current slide in Outline view.

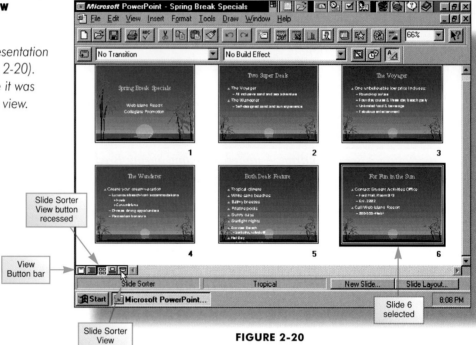

FIGURE 2-20

Because there are only six slides in this presentation and Zoom Control is 66%, you can review all slides at this time. Notice that Slide 2, Slide 3, and Slide 6 appear to need changes in line spacing. Slide 5 has text running off the bottom of the slide. Additionally, the presentation lacks pizzazz. To make the presentation more exciting, you may wish to add clip art. The next several sections explain how to improve the presentation by adding a blank line, changing slide layouts, and adding clip art.

Adding a Blank Line

The first improvement to this presentation is adding a blank line to Slide 2. In order to increase white space between paragraphs, add a blank line after the outline level three paragraph, All inclusive sand and sea adventure. Recall that a paragraph begins when you press the ENTER key and ends when you again press the ENTER key. Also recall that in a bulleted list, PowerPoint adds a bullet in front of each new paragraph. Thus, to create a blank line, you must also remove the bullet.

You can change text in both Slide view and Outline view. Recall that if you return to Outline view to add the blank line, you cannot see how the Design Template affects the text object. It is best, therefore, to change the view to Slide view so that you can see the result of editing the text object. Perform the following steps to change the view to Slide view.

Steps To Change the View to Slide View

1 **Point to the slide miniature of Slide 2 (Figure 2-21)**

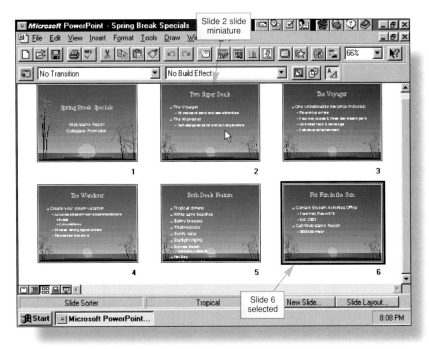

FIGURE 2-21

2 **Double-click the Slide 2 slide miniature.**

Slide 2 displays in Slide view (Figure 2-22). The Slide View button is recessed on the View Button bar.

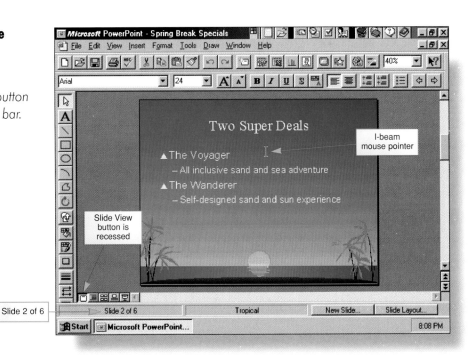

FIGURE 2-22

The next section explains how to add a blank line to Slide 2.

▶ OtherWays

1. On View Button bar click Slide View button
2. On menu bar click View, click Slides
3. Press ALT+V, press S

Adding a Blank Line to Slide 2

Now that Slide 2 displays in Slide view, you are ready to add a blank line after the paragraph, All inclusive sand and sea adventure. Perform the following steps to add a blank line.

Steps To Add a Blank Line

1 **Position the I-beam mouse pointer to the right of the second letter e in the word adventure in the paragraph All inclusive sand and sea adventure. Then click the left mouse button.**

PowerPoint selects the text object and positions the insertion point after the second e in the word, adventure (Figure 2-23). The mouse pointer displays as an I-beam when located in a text object.

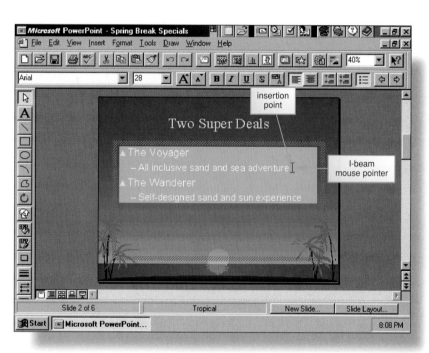

FIGURE 2-23

2 **Press the ENTER key.**

PowerPoint inserts a new paragraph (Figure 2-24). The new paragraph has the same attributes as the previous paragraph. The Bullet On/Off button is recessed on the Formatting toolbar.

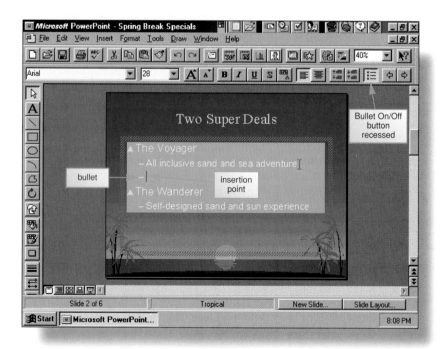

FIGURE 2-24

3 **Click the Bullet On/Off button to remove the bullet.**

The line displays blank because the bullet does not display (Figure 2-25). The Bullet On/Off button is not recessed.

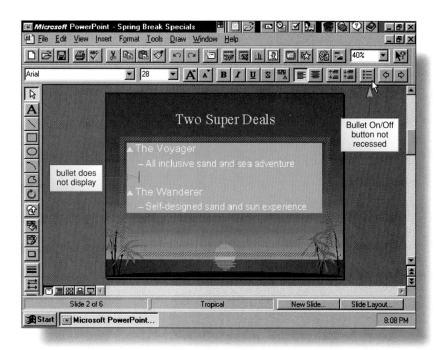

FIGURE 2-25

To display a bullet on a selected paragraph, click the Bullet On/Off button on the Formatting toolbar.

Changing Slide Layout

Recall from Project 1 that when you add a new slide, PowerPoint displays the New Slide dialog box from which you choose one of the slide AutoLayouts. After creating a slide, you can change its layout by clicking the **Slide Layout button** on the status bar. The Slide Layout dialog box then displays. Like the AutoLayout dialog box, the Slide Layout dialog box allows you to choose one of the twenty-four different slide layouts.

When you change the layout of a slide, PowerPoint retains the text and graphics and repositions them into the appropriate placeholders. Using slide layouts eliminates the need to resize objects because PowerPoint automatically sizes the object to fit the placeholder.

To keep your presentation interesting, PowerPoint includes several slide layouts to combine text with nontext objects, such as clip art. The placement of the text, in relationship to the nontext object, depends on the slide layout. The nontext object placeholder may be to the right or left of the text, above the text, or below the text. Additionally, some slide layouts are constructed with two non-text object placeholders. Refer to Project 1 for a list of the available slide layouts (Figure 1-25 on PP 1.24). The instructions on the next page explain how to change the slide layout from a bulleted list to two columns of text.

More *About* **Slide Layout**

Vary your slide layouts to keep a presentation from becoming monotonous. Choose layouts designed for one text object, multiple text objects, graphs, tables, and clip art. While varying slide layouts increases audience attention, be careful to maintain a common theme throughout the presentation by using a Design Template or color scheme.

Steps To Change Slide Layout

---

1 **Drag the elevator to display Slide 5 (Figure 2-26).**

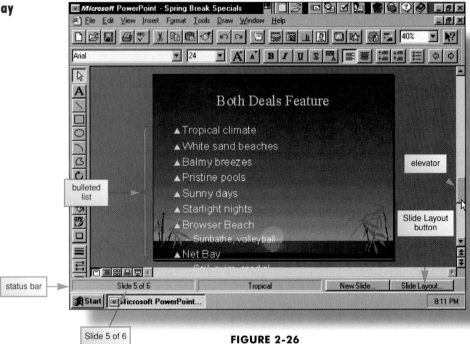

FIGURE 2-26

2 **Click the Slide Layout button on the status bar. When the Slide Layout dialog box displays, click the 2 Column Text slide layout located in the row one, column three.**

The Slide Layout dialog box displays (Figure 2-27). The 2 Column Text slide layout is selected. When you click a slide layout, its name displays in the box at the lower right of the Slide Layout dialog box.

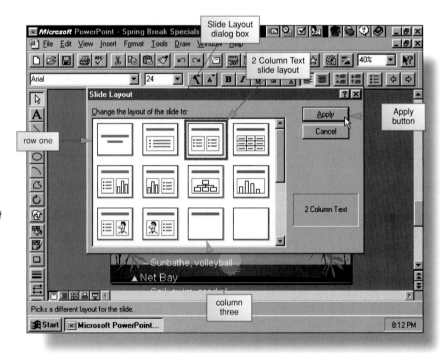

FIGURE 2-27

3 **Click the Apply button.**

Slide 5 displays the bulleted list in the left column text object (Figure 2-28). The right column text placeholder displays the message, Click to add text.

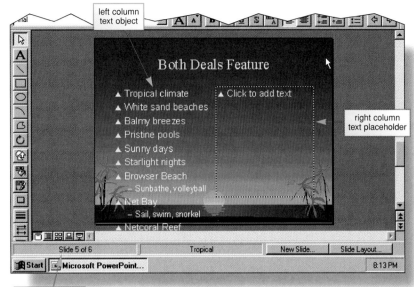

FIGURE 2-28

The text in the left column of Slide 5 is too lengthy to fit into the text object. The next section explains how to move the text at the bottom of the left column to the top of the right column text placeholder.

Moving Text

Because the bulleted list on Slide 5 contains more paragraphs than will fit in the left column text object, select a portion of the list and move it to the right column text placeholder. Perform the following steps to select a portion of the text in the left column and then move it to the right column.

Steps To Move Text

1 **Position the I-beam mouse pointer immediately to the left of the B in Browser. Drag to the right and down so that the last six bulleted paragraphs are selected.**

The six bulleted paragraphs, Browser Beach, Sunbathe, volleyball; Net Bay, Sail, swim, snorkel; Netcoral Reef, and Scuba dive, are selected (Figure 2-29).

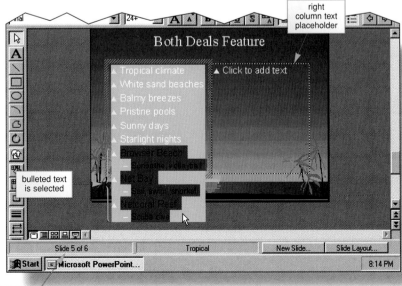

FIGURE 2-29

> **OtherWays**
>
> 1. Right-click slide anywhere except an object or object placeholder, click Slide Layout
> 2. On menu bar click Format, click Slide Layout
> 3. Press ALT+O, press L

2 **Point to the selected text. If the mouse pointer displays as a four-headed arrow, move the mouse pointer to the right of the bullets so that it is positioned over the text. Then drag the selected text to the right column text placeholder.**

As you drag the text, the mouse pointer displays as a block arrow with a small dotted box around the arrow shaft. The six selected paragraphs are moved to the right column text placeholder (Figure 2-30). When you insert text into a text placeholder, it becomes a text object.

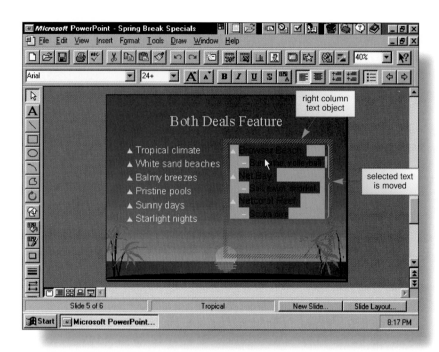

FIGURE 2-30

Recall from Project 1 that you must select an object before you can modify it.

Adding Clip Art to a Slide

Clip art offers a quick way to add professional-looking graphic images to your presentation without creating the images yourself. **Microsoft ClipArt Gallery 2.0** contains a wide variety of graphic images and is shared with other Microsoft Office applications. Microsoft ClipArt Gallery 2.0 combines topic-related clip art images into categories. Insert clip art to your presentation by selecting a clip art image from Microsoft ClipArt Gallery 2.0.

Table 2-2 gives you an idea of the organization of Microsoft ClipArt Gallery 2.0 that accompanies PowerPoint. The table contains four of the categories from Microsoft ClipArt Gallery 2.0 and a description of the clip art contained therein. Clip art image descriptions are nouns and verbs that associate an image with various entities, activities, labels, and emotions. In most instances, the description does not contain the name of the physical object. For example, an image of a magnifying glass in the Academic category

Table 2-2

CATEGORY	DESCRIPTION
Academic	Seven images: Professor Leadership Information text Communication, Meeting Communication Information, Figures Discord, Information, Focus Identify Small, Focus Investigate Identify Small, and Reward Accomplishment.
Cartoons	Ninety-three cartoon and stick people images; e.g., Reward, Worried, Problem Priority, Happy Joy Laugh, Target, Surprise, Idea Brainstorm, Planning Busy Human, Travel Human, and Fast Human.
Household	Eight images: Security Unlock, Security Unlock Solution, Cutback Scissors, Solution Band-Aid, Timeline Schedule Clock, Patience Timeline, Security Unlock Lock and Keys, and Direction.
Transportation	Seven images: Performance Fast Sports Car, Performance Ship, War Battle Powerful Battleship, Performance Fast Plane, Performance Fast War Battle Plane, Performance Fast Plane, and Priority Traffic Light.

has a description of Focus Investigate Identify Small. As a result, you may find it necessary to scroll through several categories to find an appropriate picture.

In this project you use clip art images from the Popular.pcs clip art file. Contact your instructor if you are missing clip art when you perform the following steps. A full installation of PowerPoint is required before all clip art images are available.

Using AutoLayouts to Add Clip Art

PowerPoint simplifies adding clip art to a slide by providing numerous AutoLayouts designed specifically for clip art. Recall from Project 1 that an Auto-Layout is a collection of placeholders for the title, text, clip art, graphs, tables, and media clips. When you use an AutoLayout placeholder, PowerPoint automatically sizes clip art to fit the placeholder. If the clip art is in landscape orientation, PowerPoint sizes it to the width of the placeholder. If the clip art is in portrait orientation, PowerPoint sizes it to the height of the placeholder.

Adding clip art to Slide 6 requires two steps. First, you change the slide layout to Clip Art & Text. Then you insert clip art into the clip art placeholder. The next two sections explain how to add clip art into an AutoLayout placeholder.

Changing Slide Layout to Clip Art & Text

Before you insert clip art into an AutoLayout placeholder, you must first select one of the slide layouts that includes a clip art placeholder. The clip art placeholder on the left side of Slide 6 will hold clip art. Perform the following steps to change the slide layout to Clip Art & Text.

> ◆ **More** *About*
> **Clip Art**
>
> Humor and interest are just two of several reasons to add clip art to your presentation. People have limited attention spans. A carefully placed humorous clip art image can spark attention and interest. When interest is high, it greatly increases the chance that your concept or idea will be remembered.

 Steps To Change the Slide Layout to Clip Art & Text

1 Drag the elevator to display Slide 6 (Figure 2-31).

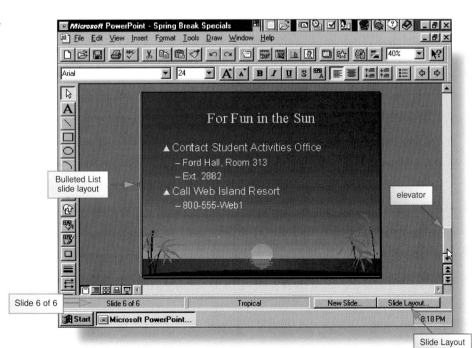

FIGURE 2-31

2 **Click the Slide Layout button. When the Slide Layout dialog box displays, click the Clip Art & Text slide layout located in row three, column two. Then point to the Apply button.**

The Clip Art & Text slide layout is selected in the Slide Layout dialog box (Figure 2-32).

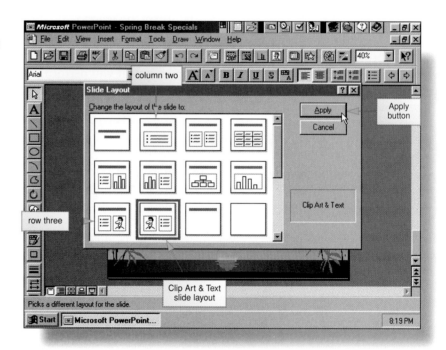

FIGURE 2-32

3 **Click the Apply button.**

Slide 6 displays the Clip Art & Text slide layout (Figure 2-33). PowerPoint moves the text object and automatically resizes the text to fit the object.

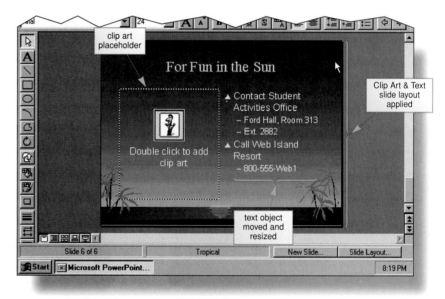

FIGURE 2-33

OtherWays

1. Right-click anywhere on slide except placeholders, click Slide Layout

2. On menu bar click Format, click Slide Layout

3. Press ALT+O, press L

You can use an AutoLayout placeholder to insert clip art even if the Auto-Layout doesn't have a clip art placeholder. For example, to insert clip art into the object placeholder of the Object AutoLayout, click the placeholder to select it, click the Insert Clip Art button, and then select a clip art picture.

Inserting Clip Art into a Clip Art Placeholder

Now that the Clip Art & Text placeholder is applied to Slide 6, you must insert clip art into the clip art placeholder. Perform the following steps to insert clip art to the clip art placeholder on Slide 6.

Steps To Insert Clip Art into a Clip Art Placeholder

1 **Position the mouse pointer anywhere within the clip art placeholder.**

The mouse pointer is positioned inside the clip art placeholder (Figure 2-34). It is not necessary to point to the picture inside the placeholder.

FIGURE 2-34

2 **Double-click the clip art placeholder on the left side of Slide 6.**

PowerPoint displays the Microsoft ClipArt Gallery 2.0 dialog box (Figure 2-35). When you open Microsoft ClipArt Gallery 2.0, All Categories is the selected category in the Categories box. The Pictures box displays clip art images by category. The selected image is a bear. Your selected image may be different depending on the clip art installed on your computer. If this is the first time you access clip art after an installation, the Microsoft ClipArt Gallery dialog box displays a message asking if you want to add clip art from PowerPoint now. Click the Yes or Add button. PowerPoint then displays the Microsoft ClipArt Gallery 2.0 dialog box.

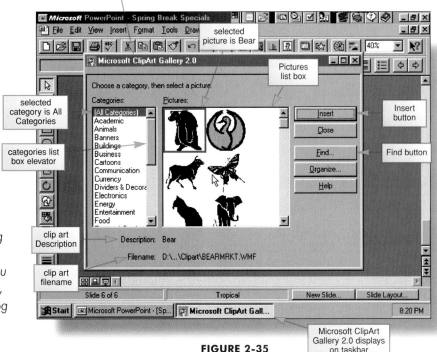

FIGURE 2-35

③ Click the Find button.

The Find ClipArt dialog box displays three boxes in which you enter clip art search criteria (Figure 2-36). The Description box is selected and contains the description, All Descriptions. Use the Description box to find clip art when you know a word from the image's description. Use the Filename containing box when you know the name of the file containing the desired clip art image. Use the Picture type box when you want to find clip art saved in a specific format.

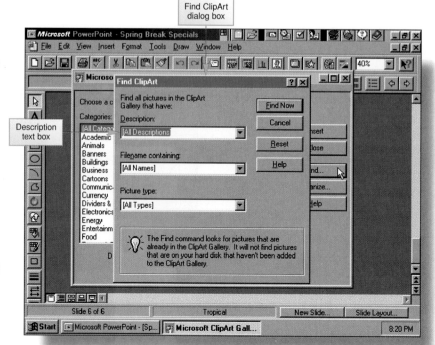

FIGURE 2-36

④ Type disappoint **in the Description box and point to the Find Now button.**

The Description box contains disappoint, which is a portion of the description, disappointment (Figure 2-37). You do not need to type the full description because the Find feature of Microsoft ClipArt Gallery 2.0 searches for all pictures containing the consecutive letters typed in the Description box. The Find Now button initiates the clip art search. The Reset button resets the Description, Filename containing, and Picture type boxes. Click the Reset button when you wish to begin a new search.

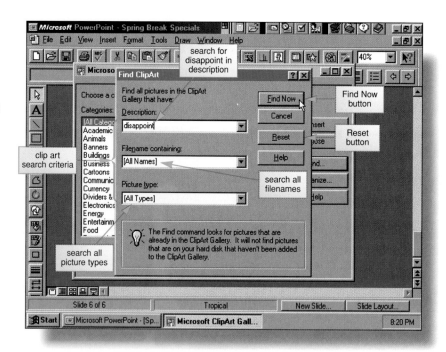

FIGURE 2-37

◆ More *About*
 Clip Art

Clip art serves a purpose in a presentation – it conveys a message. Clip art should contribute to the understandability of the slide. It should not be used decoratively. Before adding clip art to a presentation, ask yourself: "Does the clip art convey or support the slide topic?" If the answer is yes, put the clip art on the slide.

5 **Click the Find Now button.**

The Microsoft ClipArt Gallery searches for all pictures that contain disappoint in the description. All pictures that match the description display in the Pictures box (Figure 2-38). The picture of a person sitting at a desk holding a telephone receiver is selected. The selected category changes to Results of Last F(ind). Disappointment displays as the description of the selected picture at the bottom of the Microsoft ClipArt Gallery 2.0 dialog box. Your selected picture may be different depending on the clip art installed on your computer.

FIGURE 2-38

6 **Click the Insert button.**

The selected picture is inserted into the clip art placeholder on Slide 6 (2-39). PowerPoint automatically sizes the picture to a size that best fits the placeholder. In this instance, the picture is wider it is than tall (landscape orientation), so PowerPoint sizes the picture to fit the width of the placeholder. When a picture is in portrait orientation, PowerPoint sizes the picture to fit the height of the placeholder.

FIGURE 2-39

▶ *Other***Ways**

1. Right-click clip art placeholder, click Edit Placeholder Object
2. Click clip art placeholder, on Standard toolbar click Insert Clip Art button
3. Click clip art placeholder, on menu bar click Insert, click Clip Art
4. Click clip art placeholder, press ALT+I, press C

Occasionally, you find a clip art image that enhances your presentation but has a description that does not match your topic. The description is not the factor by which you select your clip art. The effectiveness of the picture determines if you add it to your presentation, not its description.

In addition to the graphic images in Microsoft ClipArt Gallery 2.0, there are other sources for clip art such as retailers specializing in computer software, the Internet, bulletin board systems, and online information systems. Some popular online information systems are Microsoft Network, America Online, CompuServe, and Prodigy. A **bulletin board system** is a computer system that allows users to communicate with each other and share files.

Table 2-3	
FORMAT	**FILE EXTENSION**
AutoCAD Format 2-D	*.dxf
CompuServe GIF	*.gif
Computer Graphics Metafile	*.cgm
CorelDRAW!	*.cdr
DrawPerfect Graphics	*.wpg
Encapsulated PostScript	*.eps
HP Graphics Language	*.hgl
JPEG Filter	*.jpg
Kodak Photo CD	*.pcd
Lotus 1-2-3 Graphics	*.pic
Macintosh PICT	*.pct
Micrografx Designer/Draw	*.drw
PC Paintbrush	*.pcx
Tagged Image File Format	*.tif
Targa	*.tga
Windows Bitmaps	*.dib, *.bmp
Windows Metafile	*.wmf
WordPerfect Graphics	*.wpg

Additionally, you can include pictures into your presentation. These may include scanned photographs, line art, and artwork from compact discs. To insert a picture into a presentation, the picture must be saved in a format that PowerPoint can recognize. Table 2-3 identifies the formats PowerPoint recognizes.

PowerPoint converts pictures saved in the formats listed in Table 2-3 by using filters. These filters are shipped with the PowerPoint installation software and must be installed before PowerPoint can properly convert files.

Inserting Clip Art on a Slide without a Clip Art Placeholder

PowerPoint does not require you to use an AutoLayout containing a clip art placeholder to add clip art to a slide. You can insert clip art on any slide regardless of its slide layout. On Slide 3, you are adding a picture of a sailboat to illustrate the type of sailing vessel used in the Voyager vacation package. Recall that the slide layout on Slide 3 is a Bulleted List. Because the Bulleted List AutoLayout does not contain a clip art placeholder, you click the Insert Clip Art button on the Standard toolbar to start Microsoft ClipArt Gallery 2.0. The picture for which you are searching is a sailing ship. Its description is Performance Ship. Perform the following steps to insert the picture of a ship on a slide that does not have a clip art placeholder.

OtherWays

1. On menu bar click Insert, click Clip Art
2. Press ALT+I, press C

TO INSERT CLIP ART ON A SLIDE WITHOUT A CLIP ART PLACEHOLDER

Step 1: Drag the elevator to display Slide 3, titled The Voyager.

Step 2: Click the Insert ClipArt button on the Standard toolbar (see Figure 2-39 on page PP 2.31).

Step 3: Click the Find button. When the Find ClipArt dialog box displays, type ship in the Description box. Click the Find Now button.

Step 4: When the Pictures box in the Microsoft ClipArt Gallery 2.0 dialog box displays the results, click the down arrow on the Pictures box scroll bar until the sailboat displays. If the sailboat is not installed on your computer, see your instructor for an appropriate replacement picture.

Step 5: Click the picture of the sailboat.

Step 6: Click the Insert button.

The sailboat displays on Slide 3 (Figure 2-40). A selection box indicates the clip art is selected.

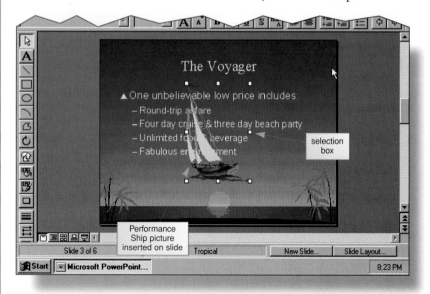

FIGURE 2-40

Moving Clip Art

After you insert clip art on a slide, you may want to reposition it. The picture of the sailboat overlays the bulleted list on Slide 3. Moving the picture to the lower right corner of the slide places the sailboat onto the water and away from the text. Perform the steps below to move the sailboat to the lower-right portion of the slide.

> **M**ore *About*
> **Clip Art**
>
> When used appropriately, clip art reduces misconceptions. If a presentation consists of words alone, the audience creates its own mental picture. The mental picture created may be different than the concept you are trying to convey. The audience better understands the concept when clip art is included.

 Steps To Move Clip Art

1 If the picture of the sailboat is not already selected, use the mouse pointer to point to the sailboat and click.

2 Press and hold down the left mouse button. Drag the picture of the sailboat down to the bottom of the slide and then to the right until the left edge of the dotted box aligns below the b in beach. Release the left mouse button.

When you drag an object, a dotted box displays. The dotted box indicates the new position of the object. When you release the left mouse button, the picture of the sailboat displays in the new location (Figure 2-41). Resize handles appear at the corners and along the edges of the selection box.

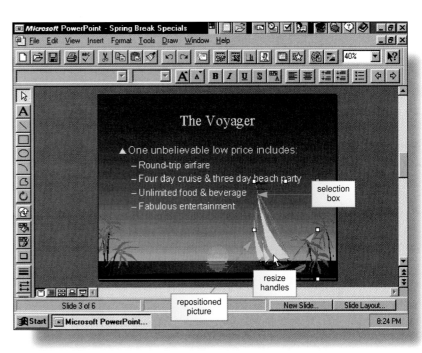

FIGURE 2-41

Changing the Size of Clip Art Using the Scale Command

You may sometimes find it necessary to change the size of clip art. For example, on Slide 3, the mast on the sailboat slightly overlaps the bulleted text. To improve legibility, reduce the size of the picture. To change the size of a clip art picture by an exact percentage, use the Scale command. The advantage of using the Scale command is the ability to maintain the aspect ratio when you resize the picture. The **aspect ratio** is the relationship between the height and width of an object. Additionally, because the Scale dialog box contains a Preview button, you can make changes and see how the picture looks on the slide without permanently changing its size. When you are satisfied with the size of the picture, click the OK button to apply the settings in the Scale dialog box. Perform the steps on the next pages to reduce the size of the sailboat.

> **O***ther***Ways**
>
> 1. On status bar click Slide Layout button, click slide layout containing clip art or media clip placeholder
> 2. Select clip art object, press arrow keys

Steps **To Change the Size of Clip Art Using the Scale Command**

1 **With the picture of the sailboat selected, click Draw on the menu bar. Then point to Scale (Figure 2-42).**

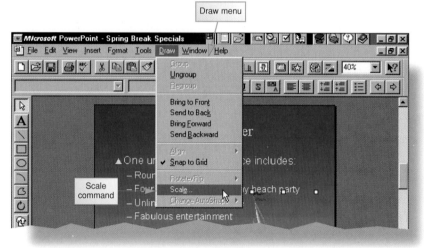

FIGURE 2-42

2 **Click Scale.**

The Scale dialog box displays (Figure 2-43). The Scale To box displays the current percentage of the sailboat picture, 99.6. A check mark in the Relative to Original Picture Size box instructs PowerPoint to maintain the aspect ratio of the picture.

FIGURE 2-43

3 **Point to the Scale dialog box title bar and drag it to the upper left corner of the slide window.**

The sailboat is fully visible (Figure 2-44).

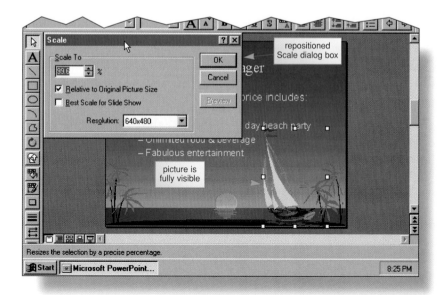

FIGURE 2-44

④ Type 85 **and click the Preview button.**

PowerPoint temporarily resizes the sailboat to 85 percent of its original size and displays it on Slide 3 (Figure 2-45). The Preview button is dimmed, or not available at this time. If the sailboat picture were still covering part of the text, you would want to try another scaling percentage to make it smaller. When you type a number in the Scale To box, the Preview button becomes available again. The OK button is used when you are satisfied with the scaling results.

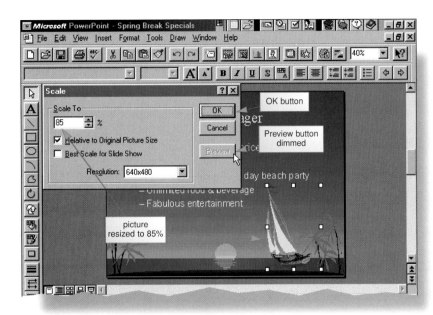

FIGURE 2-45

⑤ Click the OK button.

PowerPoint displays the reduced sailboat picture and closes the Scale dialog box (Figure 2-46).

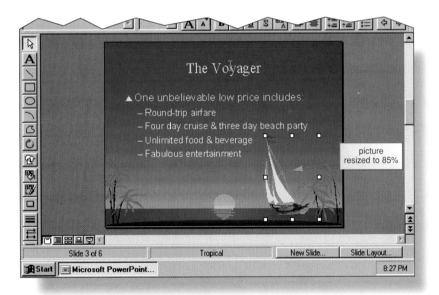

FIGURE 2-46

The Scale command is available only when a selected object displays in Slide view or Notes Pages view.

When you use the Scale command to change the size of a clip art image, the image increases or decreases proportionately to the percentage specified in the Scale To box. For example, if you wish to decrease the size of a picture to one-half its original size, type 50 in the Scale To box. If you wish to double the size of a picture (two times its original size), type 200 in the Scale To box.

Other Ways

1. Select clip art object, drag a resize handle
2. Select clip art object, press ALT+D, press E

Saving the Presentation

To preserve the work completed this far, save the presentation again by clicking the Save button on the Standard toolbar.

Adding a Header and a Footer to Outline Pages

More *About*
Headers and
Footers

Consider placing footers on slides that are used for making overhead transparencies. A slide number and presentation name help keep the presentation organized. The slide number can be a great time saver in the event you drop your transparencies.

A printout of the presentation outline often is used as an audience handout. Distributing a copy of the outline provides the audience with paper upon which to write notes or comments. Another benefit of distributing a copy of the outline is to help the audience see the text on the slides when lighting is poor or the room is too large. To help identify the source of the printed outline, add a descriptive header and footer.

Using the Notes and Handouts Sheet to Add Headers and Footers

Add headers and footers to outline pages by clicking the Notes and Handouts sheet in the Header and Footer dialog box and entering the information you wish to print. Perform the following steps to add the current date, a header, the page number, and a footer to the printed outline.

Steps **To Use the Notes and Handouts Sheet to Add Headers and Footers**

1 **Click View on the menu bar. Point to Header and Footer (Figure 2-47).**

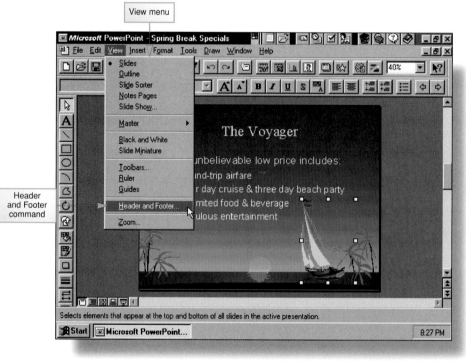

FIGURE 2-47

2 Click Header and Footer.

The Header and Footer dialog box displays (Figure 2-48). The Slide sheet displays.

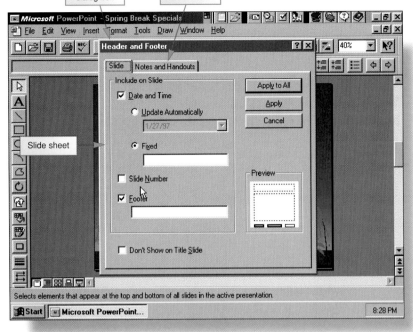

FIGURE 2-48

3 Click the Notes and Handouts tab.

The Notes and Handouts sheet displays (Figure 2-49). Check marks display in the Date and Time, Header, Page Number, and Footer check boxes. The Fixed option button is selected.

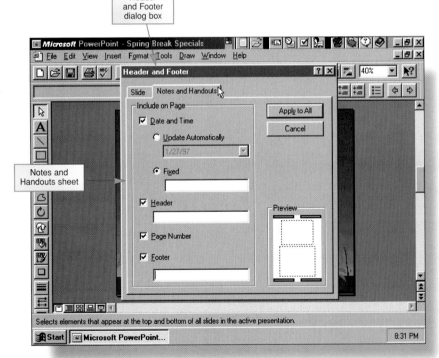

FIGURE 2-49

4 **Click the Update Automatically option button. Type** Spring Break Specials **in the Header text box. Type** Web Island Resort **in the Footer text box. Then point to the Apply to All button (Figure 2-50).**

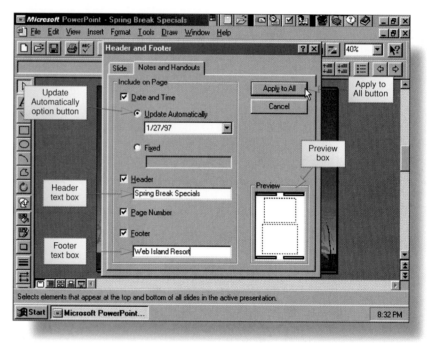

FIGURE 2-50

5 **Click the Apply to All button.**

PowerPoint applies the header and footer text to the outline, closes the Header and Footer dialog box, and displays Slide 3 (Figure 2-51). You cannot see header and footer text until you print the outline.

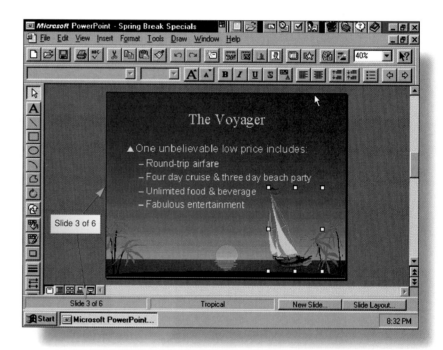

FIGURE 2-51

Checking the Presentation for Spelling and Style Errors

Now that the individual slide changes have been made, you should run Style Checker to identify errors in your presentation. Recall from Project 1 that Style Checker identifies possible errors in spelling, visual clarity, case, and end punctuation. Perform the following steps to run Style Checker.

TO RUN STYLE CHECKER

Step 1: Click Tools on the menu bar.
Step 2: Click Style Checker.
Step 3: When the Style Checker dialog box displays, click the Start button.
Step 4: Correct spelling errors and ignore correct spellings of words not located in the standard dictionary.
Step 5: If Style Checker lists visual clarity inconsistencies in the Style Checker Summary dialog box, write the slide number and the message on a sheet of paper.
Step 6: When the Style Checker Status dialog box displays, press the OK button.

PowerPoint closes Style Checker and displays the slide containing the last word not in the dictionaries, Slide 6 (Figure 2-52). This presentation contains no visual clarity inconsistencies. If Style Checker identifies any visual clarity inconsistencies, review the steps for creating the identified slide and make the appropriate corrections.

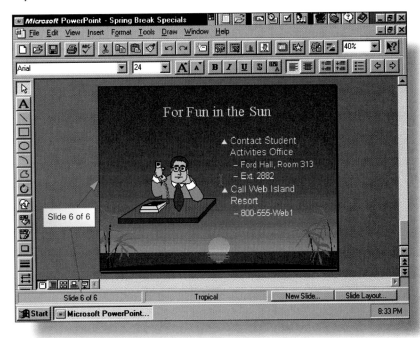

FIGURE 2-52

For more information about Style Checker, see page PP 1.40 in Project 1.

Adding Animation Effects

PowerPoint provides many animation effects to make your slide show presentation look professional. Two of these animation effects are slide transition and text build. **Slide transition effects** control how a slide displays on and exits the screen. **Text build effects** control how the objects on a slide display. The following pages discuss each of these animation effects in detail.

Adding Slide Transitions to a Slide Show

PowerPoint allows you to control the way you advance from one slide to the next by adding slide transitions to an on-screen slide show. Slide transitions are visual effects that display when you move one slide off the screen and bring the next one on. PowerPoint has forty-six different slide transitions. The name of the slide transition characterizes the visual effect that displays. For example, the slide transition effect, Split Vertical In, displays the next slide by covering the previous slide with two vertical boxes moving toward the center of the screen until the two boxes meet. The effect is similar to closing draw drapes over a window.

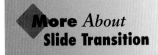

More *About*
Slide Transition

Resist the temptation to use several slide transition effects within a presentation. Too many different slide transition effects will cause the audience to focus on the visual effects and not on your topic. A general presentation design rule is to limit the number of slide transition effects to two.

PowerPoint requires you to select a slide before applying slide transition effects. In this presentation, you apply slide transition effects to all slides except the title slide. Because Slide 6 is already selected, you must select Slides 2 through 5. The technique used to select more than one slide is the **SHIFT+click technique.** To perform the SHIFT+click technique, hold down the SHIFT key as you click each slide. After you click the slides to which you want to add text build effects, release the SHIFT key.

In the Spring Break Specials presentation, you wish to display the Box Out slide transition effect between slides. That is, all slides begin stacked on top of one another, like a deck of cards. As you click the mouse to view the next slide, the new slide enters the screen by starting at the center of the slide and exploding out toward the edges of the slide while maintaining a box shape. Perform the following steps to apply the Box Out slide transition effect to the Spring Break Specials presentation.

 To Add Slide Transitions to a Slide Show

① **Click the Slide Sorter View button at the bottom of the PowerPoint screen.**

PowerPoint displays the presentation in Slide Sorter view (Figure 2-53). Slide 6 is selected. Slide 6 currently does not have a slide transition effect as noted in the Slide Transition Effects box on the Slide Sorter toolbar.

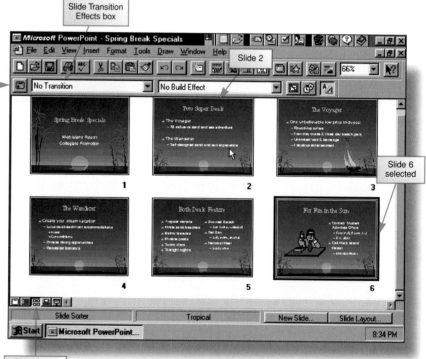

FIGURE 2-53

2 Press and hold down the SHIFT key and click Slide 2, Slide 3, Slide 4, and Slide 5. Release the SHIFT key.

Slides 2 through 6 are selected, as indicated by the heavy border around each slide (Figure 2-54).

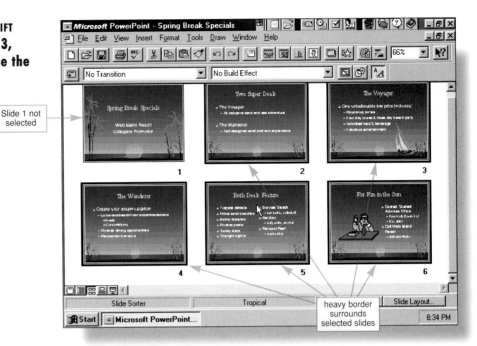

FIGURE 2-54

3 Point to Slide 5 and right-click. When a shortcut menu displays, point to Slide Transition (Figure 2-55).

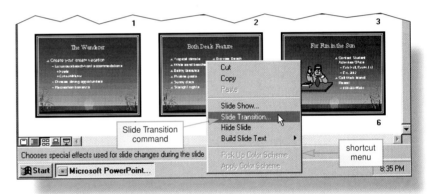

FIGURE 2-55

4 Click Slide Transition. When the Slide Transition dialog box displays, click the Effect box arrow and point to Box Out.

The Slide Transition dialog box displays (Figure 2-56). The Effect drop-down list displays available slide transition effects.

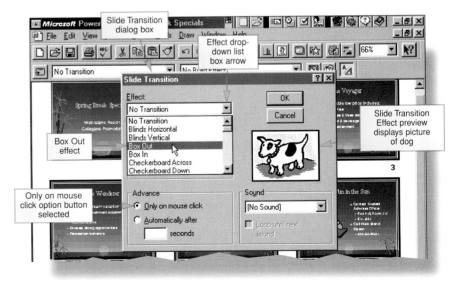

FIGURE 2-56

Click Box Out.

The Slide Transition Effect preview demonstrates the Box Out effect (Figure 2-57). To see the demonstration again, click the picture in the Slide Transition Effect preview.

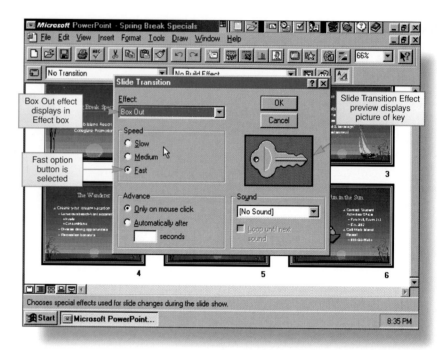

FIGURE 2-57

 Click the OK button.

PowerPoint displays the presentation in Slide Sorter view (Figure 2-58). A slide transition icon displays under each selected slide, which indicates that slide transition effects have been added to those slides. The current slide transition effect, Box Out, displays in the Slide Transition Effects box.

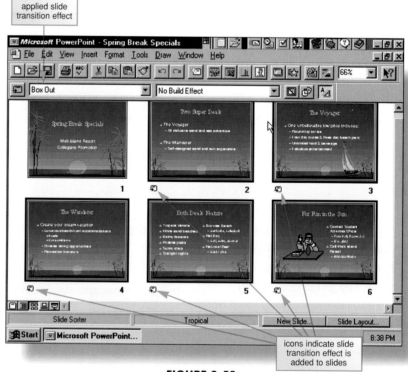

FIGURE 2-58

*Other***Ways**

1. On Slide Sorter toolbar click Slide Transition button
2. On menu bar click Tools, click Slide Transition
3. Press ALT+T, press T

Slide Sorter Toolbar

PowerPoint provides you with multiple methods for accomplishing most tasks. Generally, the fastest method is to right-click to display a shortcut menu. Another frequently used method is to click a toolbar button. For example, you can apply slide transition effects by clicking the Slide Transition Effects box on the Slide Sorter toolbar.

The Slide Sorter toolbar displays only when you are in Slide Sorter view. It displays beneath the Standard toolbar, in place of the Formatting toolbar. The Slide Sorter toolbar contains tools to help you quickly add animation effects to your slide show. Table 2-4 explains the function of the buttons and boxes on the Slide Sorter toolbar.

TABLE 2-4		
ICON	*NAME*	*FUNCTION*
▣	Slide Transition button	Displays the Slide Transition dialog box, which lists special effects used for slide changes during a slide show.
Box Out ▾	Slide Transition Effects box	Displays a list of slide transition effects. Selecting a slide transition effect from the list applies it to the selected slide(s) and demonstrates it in the preview box.
Fly From Bottom-Left ▾	Text Build Effects box	Displays a list of text build effects.
▣	Hide Slide button	Excludes a slide from the presentation without deleting it.
☞	Rehearse Timings button	Records the amount of time spent on each slide during a presentation rehearsal.
ᴬ	Show Formatting button	Displays or hides character formatting attributes.

A slide transition effect has been applied to the presentation. The next step in creating this slide show is to add animation effects to individual slides.

Applying Text Build Effects to Bulleted Slides

Text build effects are animation effects that are applied to bulleted paragraphs. This special effect instructs PowerPoint to progressively disclose each bulleted paragraph, one at a time, during the running of a slide show. PowerPoint has thirty-eight text build effects and the capability to dim the bulleted paragraphs already on the slide when a new paragraph is displayed.

The next step is to apply the Fly From Bottom-Left build text effect to Slides 2, 3, 4, 5, and 6 in the Spring Break Specials presentation. Perform the steps on the next pages to apply text build effects to the bulleted slides in this presentation.

More *About* **Text Build Effects**

Clicking the Dim Previous Points check box in the Build dialog box changes the color of the current bulleted paragraph as the next one displays. The default dim color displays in the Dim Previous Points color drop-down list box. To choose a different dim color, click the Dim Previous Points down arrow.

Steps **To Apply Text Build Effects to Bulleted Slides**

1 **If Slides 2 through 6 are not selected, use the SHIFT + click method to select them.**

2 **Right-click Slide 2. When a shortcut menu displays, point to Build Slide Text.**

When Build Slide Text is highlighted, a submenu displays (Figure 2-59). A right-pointing arrow after a menu command indicates a submenu exists. The bullet in front of the Off command in the submenu identifies the current setting.

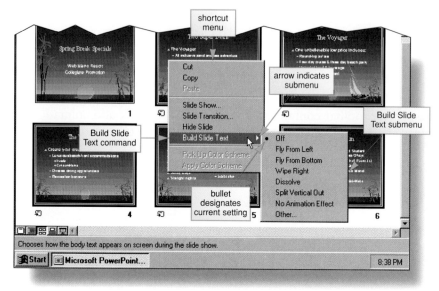

FIGURE 2-59

3 **Point to Other in the Build Slide Text submenu (Figure 2-60).**

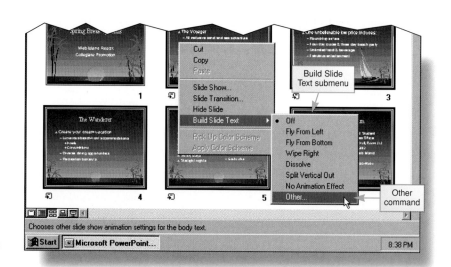

FIGURE 2-60

4 **Click Other. When the Animation Settings dialog box displays, click the Build Options box down arrow. Then point to By 3rd Level Paragraphs.**

The Build Options drop-down list displays various build options for slide text (Figure 2-61). The current build option is Don't Build as indicated in the Build Options box.

FIGURE 2-61

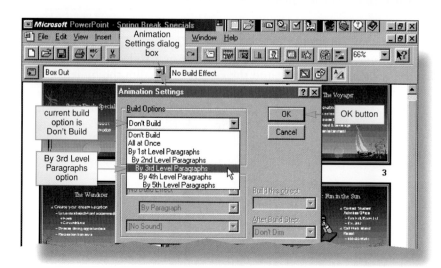

5 Click By 3rd Level Paragraphs. Click the Effects box arrow. Then point to Fly From Bottom-Left (Figure 2-62).

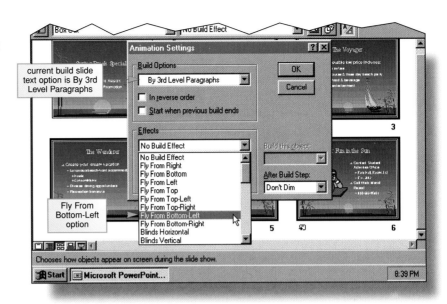

FIGURE 2-62

6 Click Fly From Bottom-Left. Then click the OK button.

PowerPoint applies the Fly From Bottom-Left text build effect to the selected slides (Figure 2-63). Fly From Bottom-Left displays in the Text Build Effects box. Icons below each selected slide indicate text build effects are applied to the slides.

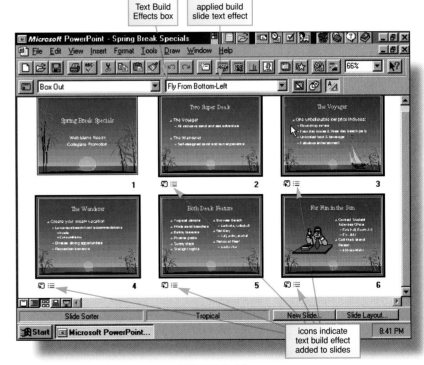

FIGURE 2-63

Slide transition and text build effects complete this presentation. You are now ready to run the presentation in Slide Show view.

Saving the Presentation Again

Because several changes have been made since your last save, you should save the presentation again by clicking the Save button on the Standard toolbar.

*Other*Ways

1. On Slide Sorter toolbar click Text Build Effects box

2. In Slide view, click Tools on menu bar, click Animation Settings

3. In Slide view, press ALT+T, press B, press letter of text build effect

Running a Slide Show with Animation Effects

Project 1 introduced you to using Slide Show view to look at your presentation one slide at a time. This project introduces you to running a slide show with slide transition effects and text build effects. When you run a slide show with slide transition effects, PowerPoint displays the slide transition effect when you click the mouse to advance to the next slide. When a slide has text build effects, each paragraph level displays as determined by the animation settings. Perform the following steps to run the Spring Break Specials slide show with animation effects.

Steps **To Run a Slide Show with Animation Effects**

1 **Click Slide 1. Click the Slide Show button on the View Button bar. When Slide 1 displays in Slide Show view, click the slide anywhere except on the Popup Menu button.**

PowerPoint first displays the Box Out slide transition effect and then displays Slide 2 with only the slide title (Figure 2-64). Recall the Popup Menu button displays when you move the mouse pointer during a slide show.

slide title

Slide 2

FIGURE 2-64

2 **Click the slide anywhere except on the Popup Menu button.**

PowerPoint displays the first Level One bulleted paragraph using the Fly From Bottom-Left text build effect (Figure 2-65).

slide title

Level One bulleted paragraph

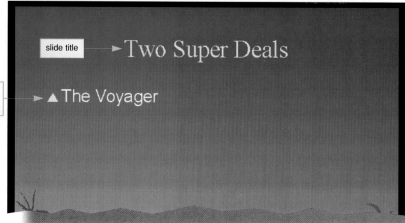

FIGURE 2-65

3 **Click the slide anywhere except on the Popup Menu button.**

PowerPoint displays the first Level Two bulleted paragraph beneath the Level One bulleted paragraph. PowerPoint again uses the Fly From Bottom-Left text build effect (Figure 2-66).

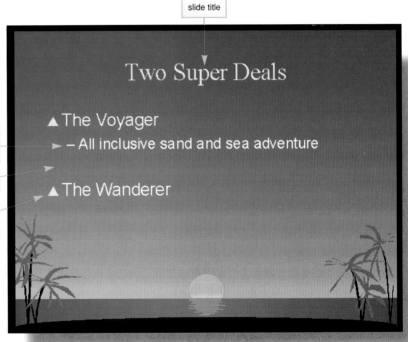

slide title

Level One bulleted paragraph

Level Two bulleted paragraph

FIGURE 2-66

4 **Click the slide two times anywhere except on the Popup Menu button.**

PowerPoint displays the blank line and the second Level One bulleted list (Figure 2-67). The first click displays the blank line. The second click displays the second Level One bulleted paragraph.

slide title

Level Two bulleted paragraph

blank line

Level One bulleted paragraph

5 **Continue clicking to finish running the slide show and return to Slide Sorter View.**

PowerPoint builds each slide based on the animation settings. When you click the slide after the last paragraph displays, PowerPoint exits Slide Show and returns to Slide Sorter View.

FIGURE 2-67

Printing in Outline View

PowerPoint allows you to print a hard copy of the current view using the Print button on the Standard toolbar. Recall from Project 1 that, while in Slide view, you click the Print button to print hard copies of the presentation slides. PowerPoint also allows you print a hard copy of views other than the current view using the Print command in the File menu. The next two sections explain how to use the Print button to print the presentation outline and how to use the Print command to print the presentation slides.

Printing an Outline

During the development of a lengthy presentation, it is often easier to review your outline in print rather than on-screen. Printing your outline also is useful for audience handouts or when your supervisor or instructor wants to review your subject matter before you fully develop your presentation.

When you display a presentation in Slide view, clicking the Print button causes PowerPoint to print all slides in the presentation. Similarly, when you display a presentation in Outline view, clicking the Print button causes PowerPoint to print the outline. The outline, however, prints as last viewed in Outline view. This means that you must select the Zoom Control setting to display the outline text as you wish to print it. If you are uncertain of the Zoom Control setting, you should review it prior to printing. Perform the following steps to print an outline in Outline view.

Steps To Print an Outline

1 **Click the Outline View button on the View Button bar.**

2 **Ready the printer according to the printer instructions. Then click the Print button on the Standard toolbar.**

The mouse pointer momentarily changes to an hourglass shape, and then PowerPoint briefly displays a message on the status bar indicating it is preparing to print the outline in the background. An animated printer icon displays on the status bar, identifying which page is being prepared to print. After several moments, the outline begins printing on the printer. The printer icon next to the clock on the taskbar indicates a print job is processing (Figure 2-68). When the outline is finished printing, the printer icon on the taskbar disappears.

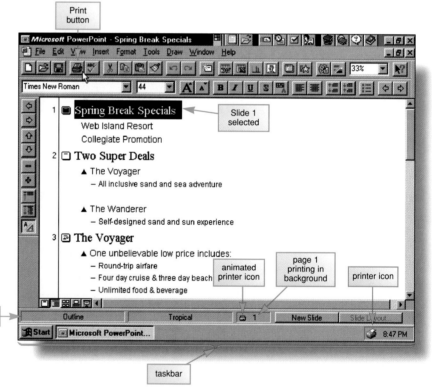

FIGURE 2-68

3 When the printer stops, retrieve the printout of the outline (Figure 2-69).

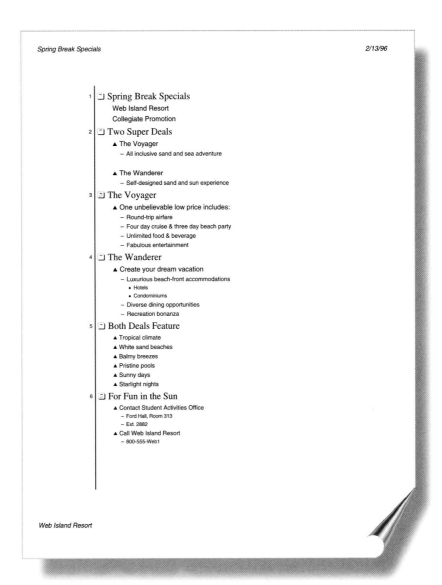

FIGURE 2-69

Other Ways
1. On menu bar click File, click Print, click Outline View in Print what box
2. Press CTRL+P, click Outline View in Print what box

Printing Presentation Slides in Outline View

After correcting errors, you will want to print a final copy of your presentation. If you made any changes to your presentation since your last save, be sure to save your presentation before you print.

Perform the steps on the next pages to print the presentation slides while in Outline view.

Steps To Print Presentation Slides

1 Ready the printer according to the printer instructions.

2 Click File on the menu bar. Then point to Print (Figure 2-70).

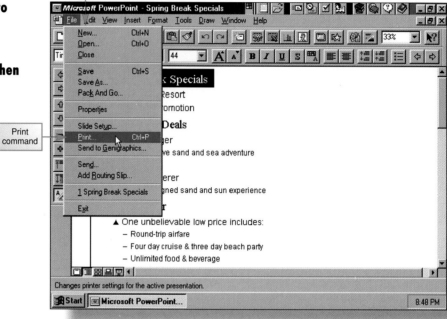

FIGURE 2-70

3 Click Print. When the Print dialog box displays, click the Print what box arrow.

The Print dialog box displays (Figure 2-71). The Print what drop-down list box displays hard copy options. Outline View is selected because it is the current view.

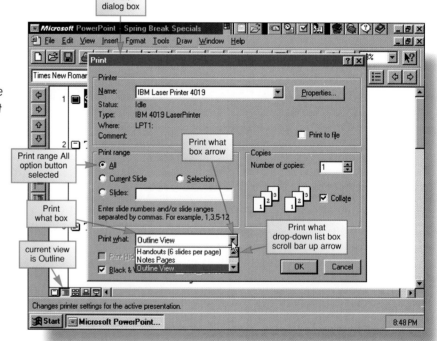

FIGURE 2-71

4 Click the Print what drop-down list scroll bar up arrow until Slides (without Builds) displays. Then point to Slides (without Builds) (Figure 2-72).

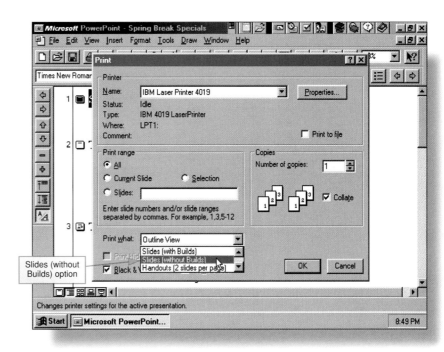

FIGURE 2-72

5 Click Slides (without Builds) (Figure 2-73).

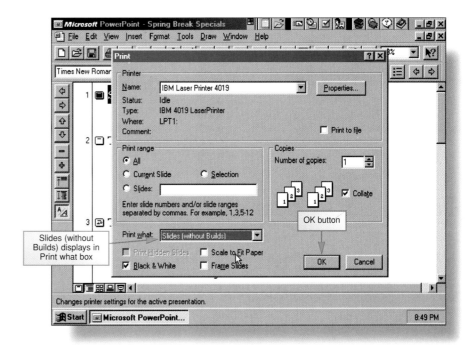

FIGURE 2-73

6 Click the OK button in the Print dialog box. When the printer stops, retrieve the printouts.

The printouts should look like the slides in Figure 2-74.

FIGURE 2-74a

FIGURE 2-74b

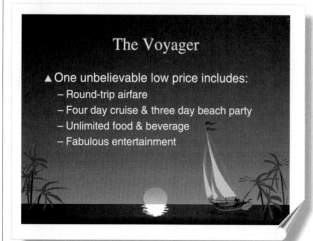

FIGURE 2-74c

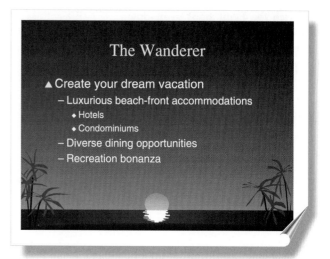

FIGURE 2-74d

FIGURE 2-74e

FIGURE 2-74f

The Print what drop-down list in the Print dialog box contains options for printing two, three, or six slide images per page. These options are labeled as Handouts [2 slides per page], Handouts [3 slides per page], and Handouts [6 slides per page]. Printing handouts is useful for reviewing a presentation because you print several slides on one page. Additionally, many businesses distribute handouts of the slide show before a presentation so the attendees have a hard copy to which to refer.

Editing a Presentation

Now that the Spring Break Specials presentation is complete, you want to review it for content and presentation flow. If you find that your slides need to be in a different sequence, you can easily change the slide order by dragging the slide to its new position. You can change slide order in either Outline view or Slide Sorter view. The following sections explain several editing features of PowerPoint. First, you will change slide order in Outline view and then in Slide Sorter view. You will also copy a slide and paste it into the presentation. Finally, you will use the Undo button to reverse the last edit action.

Displaying Slide Titles in Outline View

When moving slides in Outline view, it is easier to display only the slide titles. Displaying just the slide titles makes a large presentation more manageable by allowing you to work with one line of text per slide. The nontitle text displays as a gray line under the slide title. Showing only slide titles also prevents you from combining slides by moving one slide into the bulleted text of another. Perform the following steps to display only the slide titles in Outline view.

 Steps To Display Slide Titles in Outline View

1 **Point to the Show Titles button on the Outlining toolbar (Figure 2-75).**

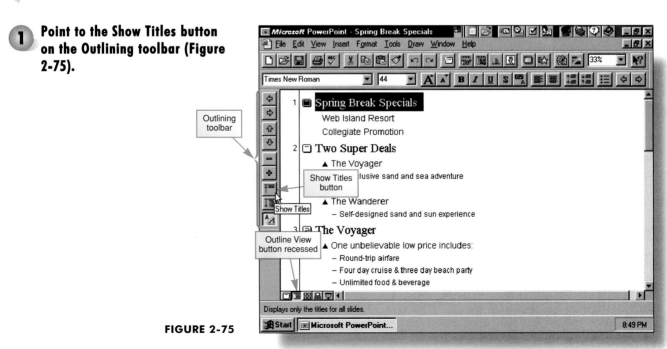

FIGURE 2-75

2 **Click the Show Titles button.**

PowerPoint compresses the slides so that only the six slide titles display in the Outline view window (Figure 2-76). Slide 1 is highlighted because it is the current slide. Nontitle text is indicated by a gray line under the title. Slides containing graphics display with graphic symbols in the slide icon.

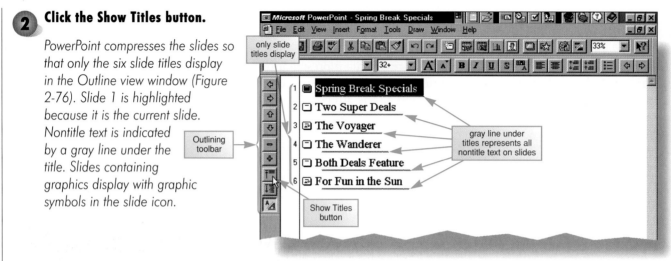

FIGURE 2-76

Changing Slide Order in Outline View

You move a slide to a new location, in Outline view, by dragging the slide icon until the horizontal placement indicator displays at the location where you want to position the slide. Perform the following steps to change slide order in Outline view.

 To Change Slide Order in Outline View

1 **Position the mouse pointer over the slide icon for Slide 5. Click the Slide 5 slide icon.**

Slide 5 is selected (Figure 2-77). The mouse pointer becomes a four-headed arrow when positioned over the slide icon.

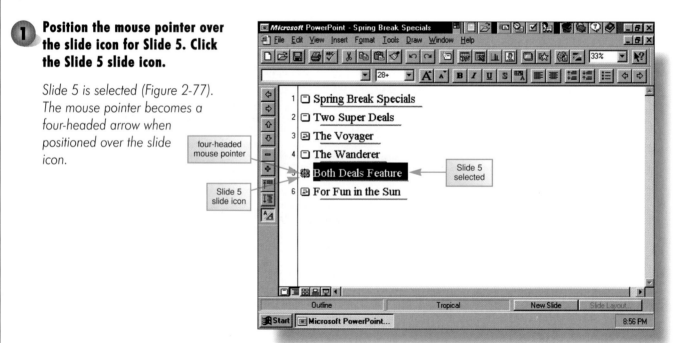

FIGURE 2-77

2 Press and hold down the left mouse button. Drag the Slide 5 slide icon up until the horizontal placement indicator displays below Slide 2, Two Super Deals, and above Slide 3, The Voyager.

The horizontal placement indicator displays below Slide 2 and above Slide 3 (Figure 2-78). The mouse pointer displays as a two-headed arrow.

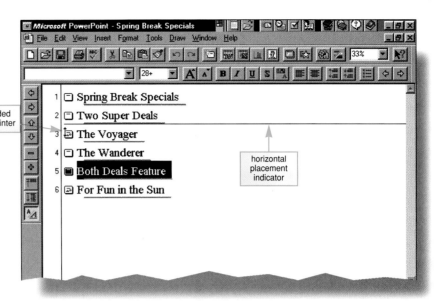

FIGURE 2-78

3 Release the left mouse button.

The slide titled Both Deals Feature becomes Slide 3 (Figure 2-79). PowerPoint automatically renumbers the slides. The mouse pointer displays as a four-headed arrow.

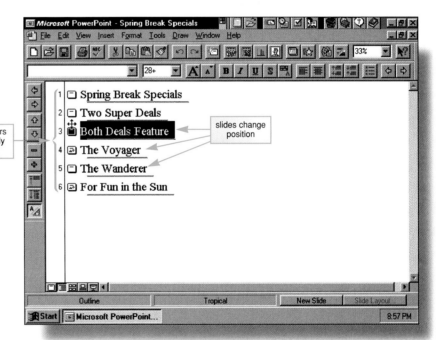

FIGURE 2-79

As you drag the slide icon, a horizontal placement indicator displays as soon as you move off the slide. The horizontal placement indicator is useful for identifying the exact location to drop the slide when changing slide order in Outline view.

Displaying All Text in Outline View

After moving slides, it is advisable to review the presentation again. Before you review the presentation, display the entire outline. Perform the following step to display all outline text.

Steps To Display All Text in Outline View

1 **Click the Show All button on the Outlining toolbar (see Figure 2-5 on page PP 2.9).**

PowerPoint expands the outline text (Figure 2-80). Slide 3 is the current slide.

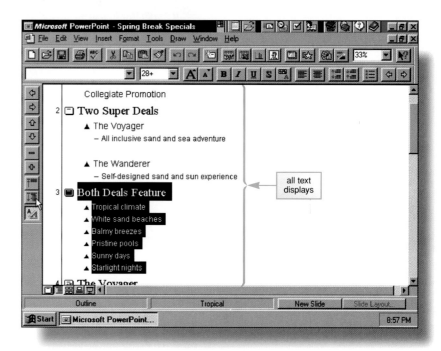

FIGURE 2-80

Changing Slide Order in Slide Sorter View

As previously stated, changing slide order in Slide Sorter view is as simple as dragging and dropping the slide into its new position. When you drag a slide to a new location in Slide Sorter view, a placement indicator displays to identify the slide's new position. The placement indicator is a dotted line. As you drag a slide, the mouse pointer displays as an arrow with a box around the arrow shaft. You move the slide to its new location by dragging the mouse pointer until the placement indicator displays at the location where you want to insert the slide. Because you cannot drop one slide on top of another slide in Slide Sorter view, the placement indicator appears to jump in front of a slide or after a slide as the mouse pointer moves around the window. Perform the following steps to change slide order in Slide Sorter view.

Steps To Change Slide Order in Slide Sorter View

1 **Click the Slide Sorter View button on the View Button bar.**

The presentation displays in Slide Sorter view (Figure 2-81). Slide 3 is selected because it was the current slide in Outline view. PowerPoint assigns a number to each slide.

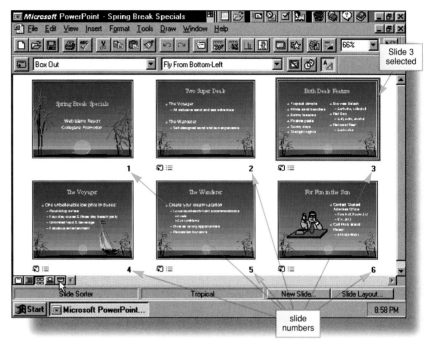

FIGURE 2-81

2 **Point to Slide 3, and then press and hold down the left mouse button. Drag Slide 3 down and to the left until the placement indicator displays after Slide 5 (Figure 2-82).**

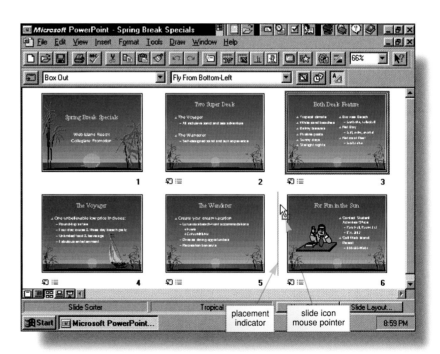

FIGURE 2-82

3 **Release the left mouse button to drop Slide 3 after Slide 5.**

Slide 3, titled, Both Deals Feature, becomes Slide 5 (Figure 2-83). PowerPoint automatically renumbers the slides.

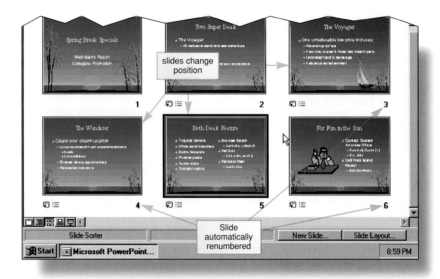

FIGURE 2-83

Copying a Slide

Occasionally you will want to copy a slide and then make changes to it. PowerPoint has a copy command that allows you to quickly duplicate a slide or any object on a slide. After you make a copy, you paste it elsewhere in your presentation. The next section explains how to copy and paste a slide in Slide Sorter view.

 To Copy a Slide in Slide Sorter View

1 **Right-click Slide 5, Both Deals Feature. When a shortcut menu displays, point to Copy (Figure 2-84).**

2 **Click Copy.**

A copy of Slide 5 is placed on the Clipboard. The shortcut menu no longer displays.

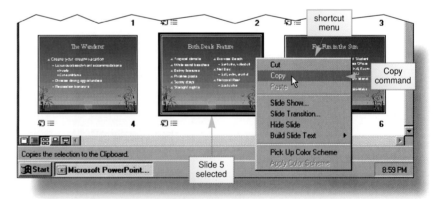

FIGURE 2-84

OtherWays

1. On Standard toolbar click Copy button
2. On menu bar click Edit, click Copy
3. Press CTRL+C

The Clipboard stores one copy at a time. If you copy another slide to the Clipboard, it replaces the first. To prevent the accidental loss of the contents of the Clipboard, immediately follow the Copy command with the Paste command. The next section explains how to paste the contents of the Clipboard into a presentation.

Pasting a Slide into a Presentation

Because a copy of Slide 5 is on the Clipboard, paste that copy into the presentation between Slide 2 and Slide 3. Perform the following steps to paste the contents of the Clipboard to the presentation.

 Steps **To Paste a Slide into a Presentation**

> ### More *About* Pasting Slides
>
> When you paste a slide, PowerPoint automatically applies the Design Template of the presentation being pasted to. For example, if you paste a slide that has the Bedrock Design Template to a presentation that has the Cheers Design Template, PowerPoint applies the Cheers Design Template to the slide being pasted.

1 **Position the mouse pointer between Slide 2 and Slide 3 and right-click. When a shortcut menu displays, point to Paste.**

The insertion point displays after Slide 2 and in front of Slide 3 (Figure 2-85). A shortcut menu displays. To reduce the possibility that you may accidentally replace the contents of the Clipboard, only the Paste and Slide Show commands are available.

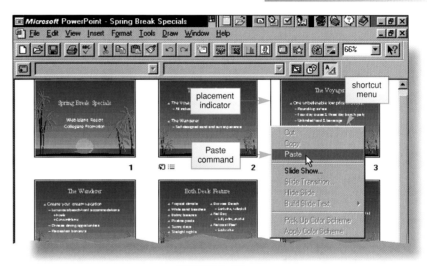

FIGURE 2-85

2 **Click Paste on the shortcut menu.**

A copy of Slide 5, titled Both Deals Feature, is inserted after Slide 2 (Figure 2-86). PowerPoint renumbers the slides. Both Slide 3 and Slide 6 are titled Both Deals Feature. The presence of the elevator in the scroll bar indicates more slides are in the presentation than can display in the Slide Sorter view window. The presentation now has seven slides because you added another slide to the presentation when you pasted a copy of the slide titled Both Deals Feature.

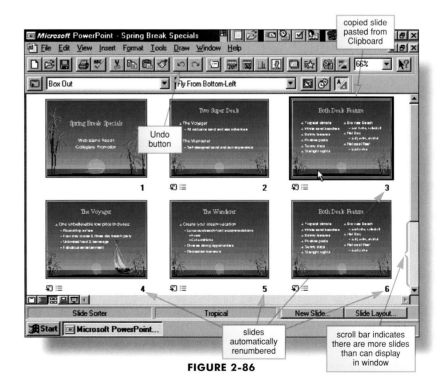

FIGURE 2-86

> *Other***Ways**
> 1. On Standard toolbar click Paste button
> 2. On menu bar click Edit, click Paste
> 3. Press CTRL+V

Using the Undo Button to Reverse the Last Edit

PowerPoint has an Undo button to reverse the last edit task. For example, if you delete an object, but realize you still want it to display, click the Undo button and the object again displays. By default, PowerPoint stores twenty edits in a buffer. A **buffer** is an area used temporarily to store data. As soon as you perform another edit task, the new task is stored in the Undo buffer. You can change the number of edits stored by PowerPoint by clicking Tools on the menu bar, clicking Options, clicking the Advanced tab in the Options dialog box, and changing the number in the Maximum Number of Undos box.

Follow the step below to use the Undo button to reverse the pasting of the copy of Slide 5 performed in the previous step.

 Steps To Use the Undo Button to Reverse the Last Edit

 1 **Click the Undo button on the Standard toolbar.**

The copy of Slide 5, previously pasted between Slide 2 and Slide 3, no longer displays (Figure 2-87). The insertion point displays where the slide previously displayed. PowerPoint renumbers the slides.

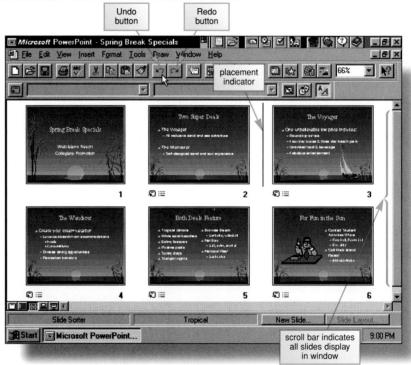

FIGURE 2-87

Located to the right of the Undo button is the Redo button. Clicking the Redo button returns the presentation to the state it was in prior to clicking the Undo button.

Saving and Closing PowerPoint

If you made any changes to your presentation since your last save, you should save it again by clicking the Save button. Close the presentation and PowerPoint by clicking the Close button on the title bar. For more details on closing PowerPoint, refer to page PP 1.37.

Project Summary

Project 2 introduced you to Outline view and clip art. You created a slide presentation in Outline view where you entered all the text in the form of an outline. You arranged the text using the Promote (Indent less) and Demote (Indent more) buttons. Once your outline was complete, you changed slide layouts and added clip art. You added slide transition effects and text build effects. Then you ran the slide show to demonstrate the animation effects, slide transition and text build. You learned how to print the presentation outline and slides in Outline view. Finally, you edited a presentation by rearranging slide order, copying and pasting, and reversing the last edit using the Undo button.

What You Should Know

Having completed this project, you now should be able to perform the following tasks:

- Add a Blank Line *(PP 2.20)*
- Add a Slide in Outline View *(PP 2.12)*
- Add Slide Transitions to a Slide Show *(PP 2.39)*
- Apply Text Build Effects to Bulleted Slides *(PP 2.43)*
- Change Slide Layout *(PP 2.23)*
- Change Slide Layout to Clip Art & Text *(PP 2.27)*
- Change Slide Order in Outline View *(PP 2.54)*
- Change Slide Order in Slide Sorter View *(PP 2.56)*
- Change the Size of Clip Art Using the Scale Command *(PP 2.33)*
- Change View to Outline View *(PP 2.8)*
- Change View to Slide Sorter View *(PP 2.19)*
- Copy a Slide in Slide Sorter View *(PP 2.58)*
- Create a Multi-level Slide in Outline View *(PP 2.13)*

- Create a Title Slide in Outline View *(PP 2.10)*
- Display All Text in Outline View *(PP 2.56)*
- Display Slide Titles in Outline View *(PP 2.53)*
- Insert Clip Art into a Clip Art Placeholder *(PP 2.28)*
- Insert Clip Art on a Slide without a Clip Art Placeholder *(PP 2.32)*
- Move Clip Art *(PP 2.33)*
- Paste a Slide into a Presentation *(PP 2.59)*
- Print an Outline *(PP 2.48)*
- Print Presentation Slides *(PP 2.50)*
- Run a Slide Show with Animation Effects *(PP 2.46)*
- Use the Notes and Handouts Sheet to Add Headers and Footers *(PP 2.36)*
- Use the Undo Button to Reverse the Last Edit *(PP 2.60)*

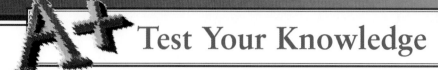

Test Your Knowledge

1 True/False

Instructions: Circle T if the statement is true or F if the statement is false.

T F 1. An outline is a summary of thoughts presented as headings and subheadings.

T F 2. Graphic objects, such as pictures, graphs, and tables, display in Outline view.

T F 3. In Outline view, the subtitle on the title slide displays on outline level one.

T F 4. The Demote (Indent more) button moves the selected paragraph up one level in the outline hierarchy each time you click the button.

T F 5. Clip art provides a quick way to add professional-looking graphic images to your presentation without creating the images yourself.

T F 6. The Scale command resizes clip art while maintaining its aspect ratio.

T F 7. PowerPoint automatically sizes clip art to fit a clip art placeholder.

T F 8. Slide view Zoom Control affects the size of text when printing an outline.

T F 9. Double-clicking a slide miniature in Slide Sorter view displays that slide in Outline view.

T F 10. Print slides from Outline view by clicking the Print button on the Standard toolbar.

2 Multiple Choice

Instructions: Circle the correct response.

1. Outline view provides a quick, easy way to _____.
   a. insert clip art
   b. change slide layout
   c. display slide miniatures
   d. create a presentation

2. To add a new slide to a presentation in Outline view, _____.
   a. click the New Slide button on the status bar
   b. click the Promote (Indent less) button until the insertion point displays at outline level one
   c. press CTRL+M
   d. all of the above

3. A presentation outline begins with a title on _____.
   a. outline level zero
   b. outline level two
   c. outline level one
   d. none of the above

4. Move a slide in Outline view by dragging the _____ to its new position.
   a. paragraph
   b. slide icon
   c. bullet
   d. none of the above

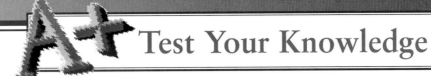

Test Your Knowledge

5. PowerPoint provides a(n) _____ button to reverse the latest edit task.
   a. Paste
   b. Undo
   c. Edit
   d. Copy

6. The presentation outline may be printed by selecting the Print command from the File menu when in _____.
   a. Notes Pages view
   b. Slide view
   c. Slide Sorter view
   d. all of the above

7. The animation effect that instructs PowerPoint to progressively disclose each bulleted paragraph during the running of a slide show is called _____.
   a. Slide Show
   b. Slide Transition
   c. Build Slide Transition
   d. Build Slide Text

8. The Scale command _____.
   a. is available in Outline view
   b. changes the size of a clip art image by a specific percentage
   c. changes the aspect ratio of the clip art image
   d. all of the above

9. Insert clip art on a slide that has a(n) _____.
   a. object placeholder
   b. clip art placeholder
   c. text placeholder
   d. all of the above

10. The horizontal placement indicator is useful for identifying the exact location to drop a slide when changing slide order in _____.
    a. Outline view
    b. Slide view
    c. Slide Sorter view
    d. all of the above

3 Understanding the Outlining View Window

Instructions: Arrows in Figure 2-88 point to the major components of a PowerPoint window in Outline view. Identify the various parts of the window in the space provided.

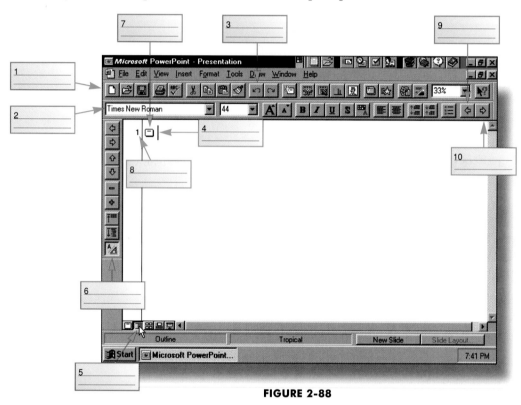

FIGURE 2-88

4 Understanding the Outlining Toolbar

Instructions: In Figure 2-89 below, arrows point to several of the buttons on the Outlining toolbar. In the space provided, briefly explain the purpose of each button.

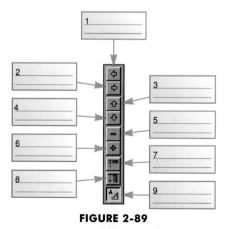

FIGURE 2-89

Use Help

1 Learning More about PowerPoint

Instructions: Perform the following tasks using a computer.

1. If PowerPoint is not already started, start a new PowerPoint presentation and select any AutoLayout.
2. Double-click the Help button on the Standard toolbar to display the Help Topics: Microsoft PowerPoint dialog box.
3. Click the Index tab. Type templates in box 1 and then double-click templates in box 2. When the Topics Found dialog box displays, double-click Using Design Templates to give my presentation a consistent look. When the Microsoft PowerPoint window displays, read the information, right-click within the dialog box, and click Print Topic. When the Print dialog box displays, click the OK button. Click the Help Topics button to return to the Help Topics: Microsoft PowerPoint dialog box.
4. Type bullets in box 1 and then press the ENTER key. When the Topics Found dialog box displays, double-click Add, change, or remove a bullet. When the Microsoft PowerPoint window displays, read and print the information. Click Change the distance between the bullet and the text. When the Microsoft PowerPoint window displays, read and print the information. Click the Help Topics button to return to the Help Topics: Microsoft PowerPoint dialog box.
5. Type trouble in box 1 and then double-click troubleshooting bullets in box 2. When the Microsoft PowerPoint window displays, read and print the I can't select a bullet information. Click the Close button to exit Help. Submit the printouts to your instructor.

2 Expanding on the Basics

Instructions: Use PowerPoint online help to better understand the topics listed below. Begin each of the following by double-clicking the Help button on the Standard toolbar. If you can't print the help information, answer the question on a separate piece of paper.

1. When in Outline view, how do you change the color of a bullet for all slides in a presentation?
2. How do you prevent a bullet from displaying?
3. How do you change the bullet character from a dot to an open file folder?
4. How do you change the size of a bullet?
5. How do you add a period to the end of every paragraph in a list?
6. How do you replace one clip art picture in a slide with another picture?
7. How do you build a slide with a clip art image that appears to fly onto the slide?

Apply Your Knowledge

1 Intensifying a Presentation by Applying a Design Template, Changing Slide Layout, and Adding Clip Art.

Instructions: Start PowerPoint. Open the presentation Triathlon from the PowerPoint folder on the Student Floppy Disk that accompanies this book. Perform the following tasks to change the presentation to look like Figure 2-90. *Hint:* Use Help to solve this problem.

1. Apply the Soaring Design Template. Add the current date, slide number, and your name to the footer. Display the footer on all slides.

2. Change the Slide Master line spacing for the First Level bullet to 0.5-lines before each paragraph.

3. On Slide 1, insert one blank paragraph after the August 16, 1997 paragraph. Insert the runner clip art image shown in Figure 2-90 that has the description, Victory Performance. Drag the runner clip art image to align the left side of the dotted box under the letter l in the word Triathlon and to display the image of the runner in the middle of the light blue pathway as shown in Figure 2-90. Decrease font size of Sponsored by: to 24 points.

4. Go to Slide 3. Change the slide layout to 2 Column Text. Move the six female categories to the right column placeholder.

5. Go to Slide 4. Change the slide layout to Text & Clip Art. Insert the trophy clip art image shown in Figure 2-90 that has the description, Goal Success. Scale the trophy clip art image to 90%.

6. Go to Slide 5. Change the slide layout to Clip Art & Text. Insert the hourglass clip art image shown in Figure 2-90 that has the description, Patience Timeline. Scale the hourglass clip art image to 95%. Change the line spacing for the First Level bullets to 1 line before each paragraph.

7. Check the presentation for spelling errors.

8. Add the Strips Down-Right slide transition effect to all slides except the title slide.

9. Save the presentation on your data floppy disk using the filename, Two-State Triathlon.

10. Print the presentation in black and white.

11. Close PowerPoint.

Apply Your Knowledge

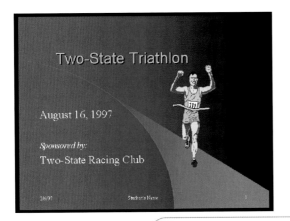

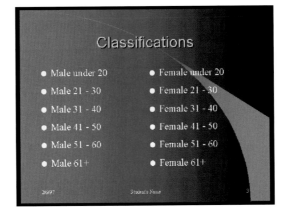

FIGURE 2-90

In the Lab

1 Adding Clip Art and Animation Effects to a Presentation Created in Outline View

Problem: You are a student in Psych 101. Your psychology professor assigns a research paper and requires you to present your findings during a five minute presentation. Your topic is having a positive attitude. To prepare for the presentation, you create the outline shown in Figure 2-91. You then use the outline to create the slide show shown in Figure 2-92. Because of your research findings, you create a unique closing slide. *Hint:* Use Help to solve this problem.

Instructions: Perform the following tasks:

1. Create a new presentation using the Cheers Design Template.

2. Using the outline shown in Figure 2-91, create the title slide shown in Figure 2-92. Use your name instead of the name Adam East. Increase the font size of your name to 36 points.

3. Using the outline in Figure 2-91, create the three bulleted list slides shown in Figure 2-92.

4. Change the slide layout on Slide 2 to Clip Art & Text. Using the clip art place-holder, insert the clip art shown in Figure 2-92 that has the description, Happy Joy Laugh. Increase the bulleted list font size to 36 points.

I.	Improving Your Attitude
	Adam East
	Psychology 101
II.	Positive Attitude Characteristics
A.	Cheerful
B.	Friendly
C.	Neat
D.	Courteous
E.	Thoughtful
F.	Considerate
III.	How to Improve Your Attitude
A.	Associate with positive people
B.	Speak well of others
C.	Isolate negative thoughts
D.	Treat others with respect
E.	Forgive and forge on
IV.	Anything is Possible with a Positive Attitude

FIGURE 2-91

5. Change the slide layout on Slide 3 to Text & Clip Art. Using the clip art placeholder, insert the clip art shown in Figure 2-92 that has the description, Consensus. Increase the bulleted list line spacing to 0.3-lines before each paragraph.

6. Drag the slide title on Slide 4 to the text placeholder. Change the case of Possible, Positive, and Attitude to lowercase letters. Increase the text font size to 66 points.

7. Add the slide number and your name to the slide footer. Display the footer on all slides except the title slide. Add your name to the outline header and your school's name to the outline footer.

8. Apply the Dissolve slide transition effect to all slides. Apply the Wipe Right text build effect to all First Level paragraphs on Slide 2 and Slide 3.

In the Lab

9. Run Style Checker to check spelling, visual clarity, case, and end punctuation. Ignore the Visual Clarity Error on Slide 4 in order to create this special effect. Correct any other errors identified by Style Checker.
10. Save the presentation on your data floppy disk using the filename, Improving Your Attitude.
11. Print the presentation outline.
12. Print the black and white presentation.
13. Close PowerPoint.

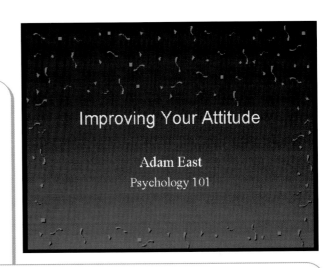

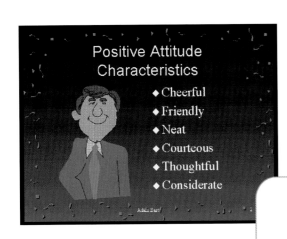

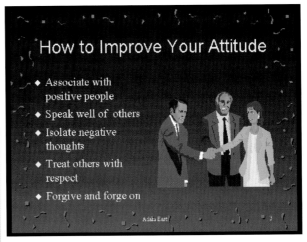

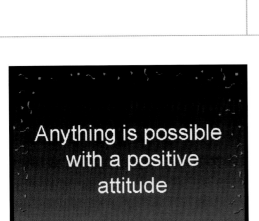

FIGURE 2-92

In the Lab

2 Using Clip Art, Slide Transition Effects, and Text Build Effects to Refine a Presentation

Problem: You are the Director of Career Development and Placement at Green Valley University. A local middle school principal has asked you to speak to his eighth grade students about career opportunities. You create the presentation using the outline shown in Figure 2-93. You then refine the presentation using clip art, slide transitions, and text build effects to create the slide show shown in Figure 2-94.

Instructions: Perform the following tasks.

1. Create a new presentation using the Splatter Design Template and the outline in Figure 2-93.
2. On the title slide, use your name instead of the name Ms. Janet Jakoby. Decrease the font size of the paragraphs, Presented by: and Green Valley University, to 24 points.
3. Change the slide layout on Slides 2, 3, and 4 to Clip Art & Text.
4. Use Figure 2-94 as a reference. On Slide 2, insert the clip art that has the description, Future Forecast. On Slide 3, insert the clip art that has the description, Surprise. On Slide 4, insert the clip art that has the description, Confusion Dilemma.
5. Add the slide number and your name to the slide footer. Display the footer on all slides except the title slide. Add your name to the outline header, and the name of the school, Green Valley University, to the outline footer.

I.	**The Future Is Yours**
	What to Consider
	Presented by:
	Ms. Janet Jakoby
	Green Valley University

II. What Is In Your Future?
    A. Education
        1. College
        2. Technical School
        3. Apprenticeship
    B. Work
        1. On the job training

III. Possible Career Choices
    A. Chef
    B. Engineer
    C. Entertainer
    D. Flight attendant
    E. Machinist
    F. Nurse
    G. Teacher
    H. Veterinarian

IV. How Do You Choose?
    A. Consider likes and dislikes
        1. Working with your hands
        2. Reading and writing
        3. Working with people
        4. Working with computers
        5. Working with animals

FIGURE 2-93

In the Lab

6. Check the presentation for spelling errors.

7. Apply the Uncover Right-Down slide transition effect to all slides. Apply the Split Vertical Out text build effect by 2nd level paragraphs to Slides 2 through 4.

8. Save the presentation on your data floppy disk using the filename, The Future is Yours.

9. Run the electronic slide show.

10. Print the presentation outline. Print the presentation slides without builds in black and white.

11. Close PowerPoint.

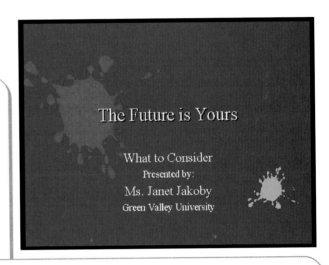

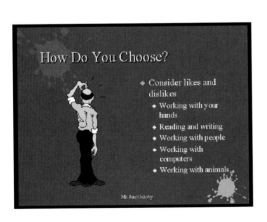

FIGURE 2-94

In the Lab

3 Animating a Slide Show

Problem: You are the sales director for Olympic Pharmaceuticals, a manufacturer of vitamins and other nutritional supplements. Experience tells you that sales are directly related to the quality of the sales presentation. Sales quotas are higher than last year and you want to make sure your sales staff understands the importance of practicing the delivery of a presentation. After much research, you prepare the outline shown in Figure 2-95. When you practice your presentation, you decide to add animation effects to the slide show. The completed slide show is shown in Figure 2-96 on pages PP 2.73 and PP 2.74.

Instructions: Perform the following tasks.

1. Create a new presentation using the Blue Green Design Template and the outline shown in Figure 2-95.
2. On the title slide, use your name instead of the name Les Deal. Decrease the font size of Presented by: to 20 points. Decrease the font size of Sales Director and Olympic Pharmaceuticals to 24 points.
3. On Slide 2, increase the font size of the Level One bullets to 36 points and Level Two bullets to 32 points. Increase the line spacing for Level Two bullets to 0.75-lines before each paragraph. Using Figure 2-96 as a reference, insert the clip art that has the description, Target. Scale the clip art to 120% and drag it to the lower-right corner of the slide.
4. On Slide 3, insert the clip art shown in Figure 2-96 that has the description, Happy Joy Laugh. Drag the clip art to the right side of the slide.

I. Polishing Your Presentation
     Presented by:
     Les Deal
     Sales Director
     Olympic Pharmaceuticals
II. Practice Makes Perfect
    A. Three key factors for a successful presentation
       1. Practice
       2. Practice
       3. Practice
III. Why Practice?
    A. Increase confidence
    B. Develop rhythm
       1. Pause for emphasis
    C. Improve articulation
       1. Vary pitch and inflection
    D. Establish timings
    E. Identify problems
IV. How To Practice
    A. Speak out loud
       1. Make a recording
          a) Video
          b) Audio
       2. Look into a mirror
       3. Find a live audience
          a) Friend or co-worker
          b) Group or team
    B. Go to delivery site
       1. Inspect equipment
          a) Audio-visual
          b) Lectern
       2. Check environment
          a) Noise
          b) Lighting
          c) Room temperature
V. Practice Makes Perfect

FIGURE 2-95

5. On Slide 4, change the slide layout to 2 Column Text. Drag the text into the right column placeholder so that your slide looks like Slide 4 in Figure 2-96. Increase the line spacing to 0.4-lines before each paragraph.

6. On Slide 5, change the slide layout to Object. Insert the clip art that has the description, Target.

7. Add the current date, slide number, and your name to the slide footer. Display the footer on all slides except the title slide. Include the current date and your name on the outline header. Include Olympic Pharmaceuticals and the page number on the outline footer.

8. Apply the Strips Up-Right slide transition effect to all slides. Apply the Fly From Bottom text build effect to Slides 2 through 4.

9. Animate the clip art on Slide 2 using the Fly From Left text build effect so it displays immediately after the slide title when you run the slide show.

10. Save the presentation on your data floppy disk using the filename, Polishing Your Presentation.

11. Print the presentation outline. Print the presentation slides without builds in black and white.

12. Close PowerPoint.

FIGURE 2-96a

FIGURE 2-96b

(continued)

In the Lab

Animating a Slide Show *(continued)*

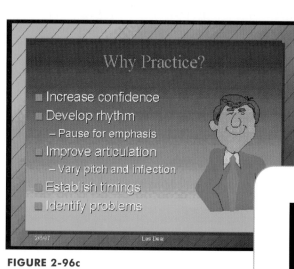

FIGURE 2-96c

FIGURE 2-96e

FIGURE 2-96d

Cases and Places

The difficulty of these case studies varies:

▶ Case studies preceded by a single half moon are the least difficult. You are asked to create the required document based on information that has already been placed in an organized form.
▶▶ Case studies preceded by two half moons are more difficult. You must organize the information presented before using it to create the required document.
▶▶▶ Case studies preceded by three half moons are the most difficult. You must decide on a specific topic, then obtain and organize the necessary information before using it to create the required document.

1 ▶ Easy Rider Limousine Service plans to show programs in local high schools to promote their prom night packages. The owner of the limousine service has outlined the presentation.

With this outline, the owner has asked you to develop slides for the presentation, using clip art and special effects to add interest. The owner also would like a printed outline that can be distributed to students at the presentation's conclusion. Use the concepts and techniques introduced in this project to create the presentation.

FIGURE 2-97

> I.   *Easy Rider Limousine Service*
>   A. *A special ride on your special night*
>   B. *Safe transportation to and from the prom*
> II. *Three Great Packages*
>   A. *The Dance*
>   1. *Secure transport at reasonable rates*
>   B. *The Promenade*
>   1. *Conveyance with an extra flair*
>   C. *The Cotillion*
>   1. *A once-in-a-lifetime adventure*
> III. *The Dance*
>   A. *Our basic package provides:*
>   1. *Terra Nova minivan*
>   2. *Courteous, licensed driver*
> IV. *The Promenade*
>   A. *Our most popular package offers:*
>   1. *Jackson World Town Car*
>   2. *Courteous, licensed driver in chauffer's cap*
>   3. *Refreshments*
>   a. *Soft drinks and hors d'oeuvres*
>   4. *Eight-speaker CD sound system*
> V.   *The Cotillion*
>   A. *Our aristocratic package presents:*
>   1. *La'Hambra Classic Limousine*
>   2. *Courteous, licensed driver in top hat and tails*
>   3. *Refreshments*
>   a. *Soft drinks and hors d'oeuvres*
>   b. *Lobster salad or prime rib sandwiches*
>   4. *Live music*
>   a. *Concert violinist performs a selection of songs*
> VI. *To experience a prom trip remembered forever*
>   A. *Call Easy Rider Limousine*
>   1. *555-EASY*
>   B. *Talk to Your High School Guidance Office*

Cases and Places

2 ▶ Phrank Ishua, director of the Ishua Institute, has outlined a presentation plugging the institute that will be given at various adult education classes and club meetings.

With this outline, Professor Ishua has asked you to develop slides for the presentation, using clip art and special effects to add interest. The owner also would like a printed outline that can be distributed to attendees at the presentation's conclusion. Use the concepts and techniques introduced in this project to create the presentation.

I. The Ishua Institute
   A. Expand physical and intellectual horizons
   B. Revelations for people of all ages
II. The Institute's Programs
   A. Training the body
      1. Practices that promote health and wellness
   B. Educating the mind
      1. Activities that enhance spiritual awareness
III. Training the Body
   A. Reach new levels of fitness through:
      1. Aerobic exercise sessions
      2. Interpretive dance
      3. Non-competitive games
      4. Rigorous isometric exercise
IV. Educating the Mind
   A. Learn to think in new ways with:
      1. Consciousness-raising workshops
      2. Alternative thought classes
         a. Extraterrestrial metaphysics
         b. Dynamics of contemplation
         c. Animated introspection
      3. Incidental meditation

V. Each Stay at the Ishua Institute Includes:
   A. Modest solitary accomodations
   B. Three nourishing meals daily
      1. Nutritionally complete fare
      2. Organically grown vegetables
      3. Salubrious confections and desserts
   C. Nightly self-examination
   D. Evening enrichment
   E. Use of extraordinary facilities
      1. Antediluvian mud baths
      2. Primeval hot springs
   F. Tours of Reflection Lake
   G. Lectures by guest instructors
VI. For a week, month, or year of rejuvenation
   A. Call Phrank Ishua
      1. 800-555-0609
   B. Write the Ishua Institute
      1. Mountbatten, WY 43721

FIGURE 2-98

Cases and Places

3 ▶▶ This summer you are working at Our Four Footed Friends, the largest pet shop in the community. The shop deals in all aspects of animal care: selling pets, providing supplies, and offering services. In addition to traditional pets, such as dogs and cats, the store peddles more unusual quadrupeds—raccoons, mongooses, wart hogs, etc. The shop stocks food, medicine, collars, grooming aids, and clothing for almost every type of pet. The store also makes pets presentable (clipping both fur and nails), supplies basic veterinary maintenance, and gives obedience classes. The workers are knowledgeable, helpful, and caring. The shop is open from 9:00 a.m. to 9:00 p.m. Monday through Saturday, and customers can call 555-PETS for information or appointments. As a break from cleaning cages, you have offered to develop a presentation marketing Our Four Footed Friends that will be exhibited at the county fair. Use the concepts and techniques introduced in this project to create the presentation. Enhance the presentation with clip art and special effects. Print an outline of the presentation that can be distributed to fair visitors.

4 ▶▶ As a well-known historian, you have been asked to develop a presentation for the International Association of Aliment Preservationists (IAAP) on the origin of canned food. You've decided to focus on two early 19th century innovators—Nicholas Appert, a wine bottler and cook, and Bryan Donkin, a one-time wallpaper manufacturer. Appert invented the canning process by placing foods in champagne bottles, corking the bottles, and then preserving the foods by boiling the bottles for varying lengths of time. The food, found to be in perfect condition after eight months, soon provisioned Napoleon's armies. Appert's methods were published in a book entitled L'art de conserver pendant plusieurs années toutes les substances animales or végétales. When Donkin's wallpaper business failed, he purchased the canning process patent and turned his idle machines to the manufacture of canned goods. Because of England's metal working industry, Donkin used tin cans (about twice the size of today's average can) instead of glass bottles. Although the canned food was lauded by the royal family and utilized on Arctic explorations, it was unpopular with the general public. The cans were expensive, in limited supply, and required a hammer and chisel to open. The trade was further crippled when some cans were found to have spoiled food. In the early 19th century the work of Louis Pasteur led to proper sterilization of food and the rebirth of the canning industry. Using this information, together with the concepts and techniques introduced in this project, create your presentation on the birth of the canned food. Enhance the presentation with clip art and special effects. Print an outline of the presentation that can be distributed to members of the IAAP.

5 ▶▶▶ While at one time most American businesses manufactured a some type of product, today an increasing number of companies instead offer a service. To be successful, service-oriented businesses must be able to clearly and convincingly explain how they can benefit prospective clients. Visit a business that provides a service and learn all you can about the service and the people to whom it is being offered. Using this information, together with the concepts and techniques introduced in this project, prepare a presentation promoting the company's services. Enhance the presentation with clip art and special effects and print an outline of the presentation.

Cases and Places

6 ▶▶▶ Visuals not only add interest to a class, they also make the class more memorable. Studies show that people recall only about ½ of what they hear, but more than ¾ of what they see and hear. Think of a lecture you have heard recently that could be improved with the addition of graphic materials. Outline the lecture's content. Use your outline, together with the concepts and techniques introduced in this project, to prepare a presentation that would augment the lecture. Enhance the presentation with clip art and special effects and print the outline of the presentation. Make an appointment with the instructor who delivered the lecture, show your presentation, and solicit comments or suggestions. Using the instructor's critique, rework the presentation. Give a copy of the presentation to the instructor.

7 ▶▶▶ In addition to Microsoft PowerPoint, other presentation graphics software packages include Aldus Persuasion, Lotus Freelance Graphics, and SPC Harvard Graphics. Visit a software vendor and try one of these, or another presentation graphics package. Use current computer magazines or other resources to learn more about the package you tested. Based on what you have discovered, together with the concepts and techniques introduced in this project, prepare a presentation comparing the package you tested to Microsoft PowerPoint. Contrast the capabilities, strengths, weaknesses, ease of use, and cost of each package. End by noting which package you prefer and why. Enhance the presentation with clip art and special effects and print the outline of the presentation.

Linking an Excel Chart to a PowerPoint Presentation

INTEGRATION FEATURE

Case Perspective

Because of the success of the spring break promotion, Mr. Hayes, your boss at Web Island Resort, decides to run the promotion every year. You suggest that he include the results of the annual guest satisfaction survey to emphasize the quality of the resort. Mr. Hayes agrees and asks you to add a slide with a chart that illustrates the high percentage of guest satisfaction into the Spring Break Specials presentation. You contact the Marketing Department for the previous year's survey results. They e-mail you a file containing an Excel worksheet and a pie chart that summarizes the results of the 1996 guest satisfaction survey. Because you know Mr. Hayes is going to use this presentation every year and the chart will change each time the survey results change, you decide to link the pie chart to the presentation. Linking the chart ensures that you always present the most current survey results.

Introduction

This Integration Feature uses the Object Linking and Embedding (OLE) feature of Microsoft Office to insert an Excel chart into a PowerPoint slide. OLE allows you to incorporate parts of documents or entire documents from one application into another. In this section, you will open the Spring Break Specials presentation created in Project 2, insert a new slide, and link the pie chart shown in Figure 1 on the next page to a new slide shown in Figure 2 on the next page. The pie chart in Excel is called the **source document** and the Spring Break Specials presentation is the **container document.**

The three most common methods of copying objects between applications are copy and paste, copy and embed, and copy and link. This Integration Feature introduces a fourth method called insert object. Use the **insert object** method when you want to insert an entire file. The insert object method allows you to insert the source file without opening the source document. In this section, you use the insert object method to link the guest satisfaction survey file to the presentation.

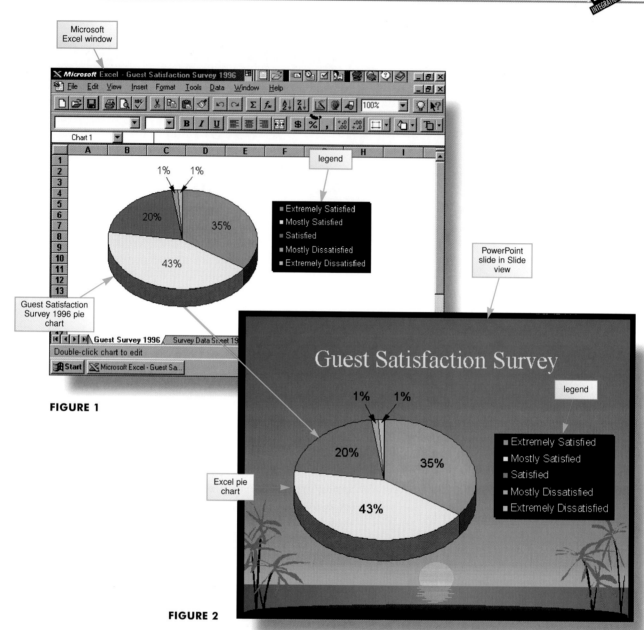

FIGURE 1

FIGURE 2

Opening an Existing Presentation and Saving It with a New Filename

To add a chart to the Spring Break Specials presentation created in Project 2, the first step is to open the presentation. To keep the original Spring Break Specials presentation intact, you save the presentation with a new name, Spring Break Specials Chart. You then add a new slide to the Spring Break Specials Chart presentation and link the chart to the guest satisfaction survey.

Before adding a new slide, first you must open the presentation. Perform the following steps to open the Spring Break Specials presentation.

TO OPEN AN EXISTING PRESENTATION

Step 1: Insert your data floppy disk that contains the Spring Break Specials presentation created in Project 2 into drive A.
Step 2: Click the Start button on the taskbar. Click Open Office Document. Click 3½ Floppy [A:] in the Look in drop-down list box.
Step 3: Double-click the presentation Spring Break Specials.

PowerPoint opens and displays the presentation in the view it was in when last saved. Project 2 last saved the presentation in Slide Sorter view.

To preserve the original Spring Break Specials presentation, you save the open presentation with a new filename. Then, you make the changes to the new presentation. Essentially you are making a duplicate copy of a file. Perform the following steps to save the Spring Break Specials presentation with a new filename using the Save As command.

TO SAVE A PRESENTATION WITH A NEW FILENAME

Step 1: Click File on the menu bar. Click Save As.
Step 2: Type Spring Break Specials Chart in the File name box.
Step 3: Click the Save button.

The Spring Break Specials presentation is saved with the filename Spring Break Specials Chart. The new filename displays in the title bar.

Creating a Chart Slide

Several steps are necessary to create a slide containing a linked Excel chart. You must insert a new slide with the Object AutoLayout between Slides 5 and 6. Next, you type the slide title. Finally, you link the Excel chart. The steps on the following pages explain how to create a slide containing a linked Excel chart.

Inserting a New Slide Between Two Slides

The slide containing the Excel chart displays after Slide 5, Both Deals Feature. Perform the following steps to insert a new slide with the Object AutoLayout.

TO INSERT A NEW SLIDE

Step 1: Click between Slide 5 and Slide 6.
Step 2: Click the New Slide button on the status bar.
Step 3: When the New Slide dialog box displays, scroll down to display the Object AutoLayout. Double-click the Object AutoLayout.

PowerPoint inserts a slide after Slide 5, numbers the new slide as Slide 6 and renumbers the original Slide 6 as Slide 7 (Figure 3 on the next page). Slide 7 is not visible in Figure 3.

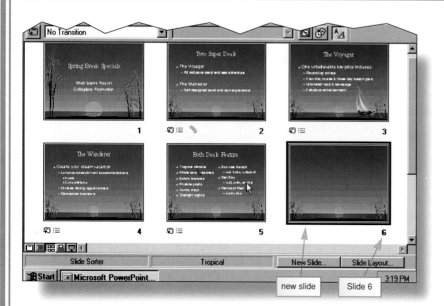

FIGURE 3

Typing a Slide Title

The next step is to type the slide title. The chart represents the results of the guest satisfaction survey. The slide title, therefore, is Guest Satisfaction Survey. Before typing, you must change views. Perform the following steps to type the slide title.

TO TYPE A SLIDE TITLE

Step 1: Double-click Slide 6 to display the slide in Slide view.

Step 2: Type Guest Satisfaction Survey in the title placeholder.

The slide title for Slide 6 displays.

◆ **More** *About*
Linked Objects

When the name or location of a source document changes, you must reconnect the link. Click the linked object and then click Links on the Edit menu. In the Links box, click the source document, click the Change Source button, and select the renamed or moved source document. Click the Update Now button.

Linking an Excel Chart to a Presentation

The Web Island Resort Marketing Department created the chart from the results of the 1996 Guest Satisfaction Survey. You link the existing chart to Slide 6 so the chart always reflects the current survey results. The Student Floppy Disk contains the chart, Guest Satisfaction Survey 1996, in the PowerPoint folder. Perform the following steps to link the Excel chart to Slide 6 in the Spring Break Specials Chart presentation.

Steps To Link the Excel Chart to Slide 6

1 **Remove your data floppy disk from drive A. Insert the Student Floppy Disk that accompanies this book into drive A. Double-click the Object placeholder on Slide 6.**

The Insert Object dialog box displays (Figure 4). Create New is the default. AutoSketch is selected as the default object type. The default object type on your computer may be different depending on options selected during the installation of Microsoft Office 95.

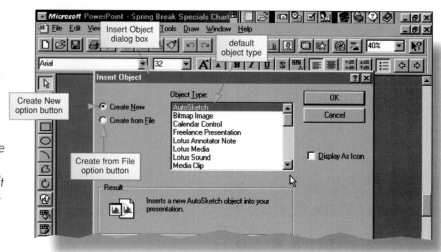

FIGURE 4

2 **Click Create from File. Point to the Browse button (Figure 5).**

3 **Click the Browse button. When the Browse dialog box displays, double-click the PowerPoint folder. Click Guest Satisfaction Survey.**

The Guest Satisfaction Survey file is highlighted in the Name box.

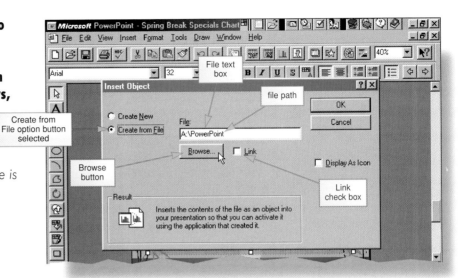

FIGURE 5

4 **Click the OK button. When the Insert Object dialog box displays, click Link.**

The File text box displays the path, or location, of the Excel chart (Figure 6). The check mark in the Link check box indicates the file listed in the File text box will be linked to the presentation.

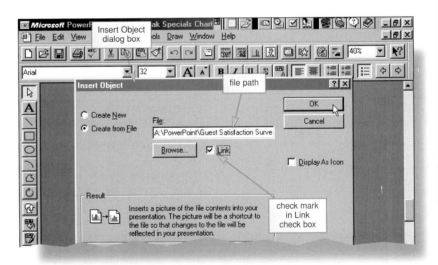

FIGURE 6

5 **Click the OK button.**

PowerPoint automatically sizes and displays the chart to fit the Object placeholder on Slide 6 (Figure 7). PowerPoint links the Customer Satisfaction Survey 1996 file, located on the Student Floppy Disk in drive A, to the presentation.

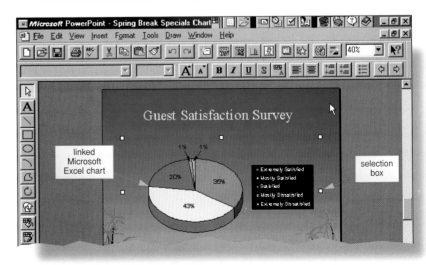

FIGURE 7

When you click Create from File in the Insert Object dialog box, the dialog box changes (Figure 5 on page PPI 1.5). The Object Type list box no longer displays and is replaced by the File text box. Another change to the dialog box is the Link check box. The **Link** check box inserts the object as a linked object. A **linked object** maintains a connection to its source. If the original object changes, the linked object on the slide also changes. The linked object itself is stored in the source file where it was created, not in the presentation.

For example, the Excel chart you inserted into the slide is stored in the Guest Satisfaction Survey file on the Student Floppy Disk. Because you linked the Guest Satisfaction Survey file to the presentation, the Guest Satisfaction Survey file changes to display automatically on the chart on Slide 6. The PowerPoint presentation stores a representation of the original Guest Satisfaction Survey file and information about its location. Later, if you move or delete the source file, the link is broken and the object is not available.

Now that the linked pie chart displays on Slide 6, you want to improve the readability of the chart by increasing its size. The next section explains how to increase the size of the chart to best fit the slide.

Scaling a Linked Object

Increasing the size of the pie chart on Slide 6 improves the readability of the chart and improves the overall appearance of the slide. You increase the size of the pie chart using the Scale command on the Draw menu. Recall from Project 2 that the Scale command maintains the aspect ratio of the object. Perform the following steps to increase the size of the pie chart.

TO SCALE A LINKED OBJECT

Step 1: If not already selected, click the pie chart.
Step 2: Click Draw on the menu bar. Click Scale.
Step 3: Type 200 and then press the ENTER key. Click the OK button.

PowerPoint resizes the chart. PowerPoint limits the scaling percentage to the maximum height or width of a slide. The chart, therefore, is limited to 187.1 percent instead of 200 percent because of the width of the slide.

The changes to Slide 6 are complete. The next section explains how to save and print the linked presentation.

Saving and Printing a Linked Presentation

Perform the following steps to save and then print the Spring Break Specials Chart presentation.

TO SAVE AND PRINT A LINKED PRESENTATION

Step 1: Click the Save button on the Standard toolbar.
Step 2: Click the Print button on the Standard toolbar.

Summary

This Integration Feature introduced you to linking an object to a presentation. First, you opened an existing presentation, saved it with a new filename, and inserted a new slide onto which the chart from Excel was linked. Then, you performed the linking process. When you open a linked presentation, the object linking and embedding function of Microsoft Office 95 opens the presentation and updates the link to the chart file, providing the most current version of the chart. Next, you scaled the linked object to improve the readability. Finally, you saved and printed the linked presentation.

What You Should Know

Having completed this Integration Feature, you should be able to perform the following tasks:

▶ Insert a New Slide *(PPI 1.3)*
▶ Link the Excel Chart to Slide 6 *(PPI 1.4)*
▶ Open an Existing Presentation *(PPI 1.3)*
▶ Save a Presentation with a New Filename *(PPI 1.3)*

▶ Save and Print a Linked Presentation *(PPI 1.6)*
▶ Scale a Linked Object *(PPI 1.6)*
▶ Type a Slide Title *(PPI 1.4)*

In the Lab

1 Using Help

Instructions: Perform the following tasks using a computer.

1. Start PowerPoint. Double-click the Help button on the Standard toolbar to display the Help Topics: Microsoft PowerPoint dialog box.
2. Click the Answer Wizard tab. Type ole in box 1 and then click the Search button. In the Tell Me About section in box 2, double-click Exchanging information with other applications. Read the Help information about Sharing information, Linking information, and Embedding objects. Click the Help Topics button.
3. Click the Search button in the Help Topics: Microsoft PowerPoint dialog box. In the Tell Me About section, double-click Updating a link. Read and print the Help information. Click the Help Topics button.
4. Type linked objects in box 1 and then click the Search button. In the How Do I section, double-click Update a link manually. Read and print the Help information. Click the Help Topics button.
5. Click the Search button. In the How Do I section, double-click Reconnect links to renamed or moved documents. Read and print the Help information. Click the Close button.
6. Label each printout with your name. Submit the printouts to your instructor.

In the Lab

2 Linking a 3-D Bar Chart to a Slide

Problem: You are the general manager of Vacation Vistas travel agency applying for a short-term loan to cover operating expenses. The bank requests that you present an analysis of your first-quarter expenses, both budgeted and actual. Wanting to appear professional, you create a PowerPoint slide show. Knowing the bank will request this analysis again, you link the chart to the presentation.

Instructions: Perform the following tasks.
1. Open the document, Vacation Vistas, from the PowerPoint folder on the Student Floppy Disk that accompanies this book.
2. On Slide 2, link the file, Expense Comparison 1st Quarter 1997, located in the PowerPoint folder on the Student Floppy Disk. Scale the chart to 150%. Center the chart on the slide.
3. Add your name in the footer on all slides.
4. Save the presentation as Vacation Vistas Budget on your data floppy disk. Print the presentation in black and white. Close PowerPoint.

3 Linking Two-Column Charts to a Presentation

Problem: Your manager at Mega-Money Management, Mr. Richard Rich, conducts weekly investment seminars at which he displays Excel charts to illustrate his topic. He recently learned that you could create a PowerPoint presentation and link his Excel charts. He asks you to create a PowerPoint presentation and link two Excel charts to illustrate this week's topic, Risky Money.

Instructions: Perform the following tasks.
1. Open the document, Risk, from the PowerPoint folder on the Student Floppy Disk that accompanies this book.
2. Use the Large Object AutoLayout and insert a new slide after Slide 2. Link the file, Secured Fund, located in the PowerPoint folder on the Student Floppy Disk. Scale the chart to 170%. Center the chart on the slide.
3. Use the Large Object AutoLayout and insert a new slide after Slide 3. Link the file, Index 500 Stock, located in the PowerPoint folder on the Student Floppy Disk. Scale the chart to 170%. Center the chart on the slide.
4. Add your name in the footer on all slides.
5. Save the presentation as Risky Money on your data floppy disk. Print the presentation in black and white. Close PowerPoint.